the schools
next time

"God gave Noah the rainbow sign,
No more water, the fire next time!"

the schools
next time

Explorations in
Educational Sociology

donald r. thomas

Chairman, Department of Education
The American University, Washington, D.C.

mcgraw-hill book company

New York   San Francisco   St. Louis   Düsseldorf   Johannesburg
Kuala Lumpur   London   Mexico   Montreal   New Delhi
Panama   Rio de Janeiro   Singapore   Sydney   Toronto

This book was set in Helvetica Light by Black Dot, Inc. The editors were Robert C. Morgan and Judith Chaffin, the designer was Janet Durey Bollow, and the production supervisor was Michael A. Ungersma.

The printer and binder was The Murray Printing Company.

the schools next time
Explorations in Educational Sociology

Printed in the United States of America.

Library of Congress Cataloging in Publication Data

Thomas, Donald R.
  The schools next time.
  Bibliography: p.
  1. Educational sociology. I. Title.
LC191.T52   370.19'3   72-8806
ISBN 0-07-064245-1

LC
191
.T52

1234567890   MUMU   79876543

to my mother,
lillian, whose middle name
has always been hope

contents

preface

Some years ago, Louis Fischer and I wrote a book called *The Social Foundations of Educational Decisions*. We tried to be reasonably comprehensive, temporally relevant, and academically objective. We learned that such an assignment was not easily accomplished. First, one man's version of comprehensiveness is another man's vision of narrowness. Second, the ebb and flow of events make relevancy an elusive quarry. Finally, every man is a captive of his own experience and perceptions. His viewpoint can never be hidden; it is embedded even in his seemingly most indifferent observations.

In this book I have not attempted a comprehensive survey of the whole field of educational sociology. Rather, I have looked at some specific issues that seemed to need special attention, either because they had been largely overlooked in current writing or because new data warranted amending present thought on them. Certainly I bring to these issues a different perspective, one that is both personal and contemporary; however, I have made no attempt to produce eternal truths. The future erosion of the views presented in this book is anticipated with neither alarm nor regret.

Inevitably, such material as this is fugitive. What is said here in July of 1972 may need amendment by the snows of Christmas. The results of the Presidential election, current Supreme Court decisions, further data and study of the 1970 census, and a host of other events in our ever-changing society, could modify any one of a number of my observations and conclusions. But eventually one must stop to scratch out a benchmark, take a stand, and say that here and now, this is what I think. This is what I have done.

Traditional expressions of gratitude here should be mostly awarded to students, both undergraduate and graduate, without whom no teacher could survive. It is their stimulation and challenge, their incredible hope and sense of mission, that sustains. Like an actor or a writer or a poet, a teacher is grateful for the approval of his professional colleagues, but it is his audience, his students, with whom he must ultimately succeed. He is always in their debt.

Specifically, I want to acknowledge and thank members of my Case Western Reserve University 1970 seminar on school organization: Andrea Rosenberg, Allan Rosenfield, Robert Brownlee, Tom Malloy, and Ann Petersen, all of whom were unafraid to confront hard issues and new thoughts. Also I want to acknowledge and thank Father Jim Leehan, Phil Speser, and the host of others of the "Kent State Days" at C.W.R.U. who taught me so much about the "new" culture. And may I acknowledge my debt to the wisdom of certain men in education: Richard Foster, John Stanavage, Merle Borrowman, Art Pearl, Dirck Brown, Allen Fonoroff, and Louis Fischer. Finally, I have enjoyed many productive associations with colleagues in a wide variety of disciplines, with associates from many professional fields, and with innumerable school people, all of whom have contributed to my thinking.

Most of all, I want to thank my wife, Sarah, who sustains me, and my children, Jordan, Lanny, Melinda, David, and Julie, who make it all worthwhile.

d. r. t.

**the schools
next time**

introduction

Public education in America is in trouble. The rages and discontents that now fill the air with cries of revolution, crisis, despair, and reform are not strangers to this vital social institution. American education has always operated in arenas of dissent, discord, and debate. But it has survived, and possibly it will live again, because American society cannot and, it is hoped, will not abandon public education, no matter what its present and multiple deficiencies. *There must be change this time,* however, and perhaps even reform, because the present disorders involve so many fundamental issues.

1

The educational sociologists are the monitors, the interpreters, and the forecasters of relations between society and the schools, and in these roles can pinpoint those areas of greatest tension and stress. It is the purpose of this book to say: Look here, this is where the fissure is too great; watch the boiling point in this area; here is an eruption that needs attending to at once, a spasm that cannot continue to be ignored. This is a book about some educational storm centers, old and new, and what possibly can be done to respond to their challenges.

The focus of education today is, of course, the city and its suburbs. How the cities evolved and how their education was conceived and developed have been powerful determinants of today's urban educational problems. Racism, the competitive ethic, and suburban colonialism are but a few of the important factors one must consider when confronting the issues of equal educational opportunity, integration, bilingual-biculturalism, the outright oppression of minority groups, and the need to recognize finally the realities of a culturally pluralistic society.

Urban schools are "out of it." The corporate single-product model (the Dick and Jane syndrome) is outmoded and dysfunctional, just as school organizational schemes are misapplied and little understood. Democracy in urban education is a value little used and often feared. Problems such as community participation and control, the misuse or nonuse of organizational theory, and the revolt of the youth culture must be examined.

Forecasting the future requires new skills, new perspectives, and perhaps new hopes. What is the role of demography in educational planning? Will the political socialization techniques presently used in schools continue to breed rebellion? If the past is indeed prelude to the future, what had happened in earlier times when we attempted educational reform? What about the future of organized educators themselves? Where are they going and with what possible consequences, both negative and positive? Indeed, is there really such a thing as an education profession? Does society recognize it? Do educators really know what they want from society? And does society know what it wants from education? What do educators want for themselves? What do they want from a whole new generation of young people born in the turmoil of jets, TV, drugs, war, and constant domestic conflict?

Perhaps never before in American educational history has there been so urgent a need for systematic study of the complex interpenetrations of the schools and the society. What can be done about what Ralph Waldo Emerson called our "system of despair"? Have we reached the point of final choice implied in the grim warning "No more water, the fire next time!"? Or is there still some hope for the schools next time?

chapter one

what is
educational sociology?

I would like to reopen the issue of educational sociology. Nothing much has been said about it these past few years. I am writing from the bridge between education and sociology, because I still insist upon the independence of education and sociology and the need for bridges.

A bridge connects two points, two sides, two autonomous perspectives of the world. It can serve both sides in the commerce of ideas. A person standing on a bridge has a view, a perspective unavailable to the residents of either bank; he can see both and call attention to the qualities of each that the other could not know or, at least, does not seem to understand.

My use of the term *educational sociology* rather than *sociology of education* is deliberate. The issue of educational sociology versus the sociology of education can hardly compare to the Arab-Israeli dispute, the war in Vietnam, the high cost of living, or the air and water pollution controversies as one of the crucial social debates of our time. On the other hand, it is not simply a case of semantic or academic nit-picking. The difference in terms has tended to dominate all considerations of an appropriate content and primary perspective for the bridge between the fields of education and sociology.

It is clear that *sociology* is now an accepted social science. Colleges, universities, and even some high schools consider it an area of investigation essential to assuring their accreditation. It has not always been clear, however, just what the legitimate and scientific concerns of sociology are, since it apparently can overlap a variety of other disciplines, each of which jealously guards its alleged exclusive contribution to knowledge. It is less clear that *education* is a social science or even a discipline, but as a constant quasi-professional activity, its concerns and content are relatively well known. The distinction between a discipline and a quasi-professional activity is one that plagues social work, law, medicine, and other so-called applied science fields of endeavor. Assessing education would produce similar equivocal answers.

The problem may be stated in another way. Can an established field of social science find happiness in the workaday world of education, or vice versa? Obviously, this has not been a compelling human drama, for both fields of sociology and education continue to exist and function, and neither seems overly concerned about the ambiguity of its relationships with the other.

This volume was written for both the student of education and the student of sociology. In accord with my admitted bias that the needs and concerns of education are primary, the word *educa-*

tional precedes the word *sociology*. But I want to emphasize that the field of sociology provides the educator with a set of materials that are useful and perhaps vital to the examination and solution of educational problems. The thrust of my perspective is in its *intent*. Educational sociologists can be concerned about building a store-house of sociological content, but they must first insist on using these resources. It is entirely possible that the field of educational sociology may produce some valid and useful sociological theory; such outcomes would be logical, though they may not be spectacular. But educational sociology is more a field of study that attempts, in behalf of both educational practitioners and sociologists, to *monitor* the multivariate and ever-changing relationships between education and the general society, using sociological tools and techniques. It serves, at once, as a broker, go-between, voyeur, counselor, negotiator, envoy, jobber, translator, and interpreter. It may provide data or theory either to education or to sociology, but its *raison d'être* is the creation of a bridge between them, a solid connecting link.

As such, the field of educational sociology is, I suppose, more functional than philosophical. It is most often applied, in the sense that its insights and data are utilized to relate more to real rather than theoretical problems. As will be demonstrated, it can recommend educational policies by identifying social issues both in the schools and in the social environment that may imply relation-ships and therefore educational problems. It can answer crucial needs for systematically gathered data on aspects of problems that educators have neither the time nor inclination to investigate. On rare occasions, its activity may even provoke educational change. Conversely, I hope, it can jar sociological theory with reality, provide the sociologist with mountains of useful data, and contribute to that discipline the challenge of dealing with what may be a most special and interesting case in human affairs.

Educational sociology is a broad field when examined in the tradition of such sociological thinkers as Comte, Durkheim,

Ward, or Small. It includes materials that, in some quarters, might be more appropriately assigned to anthropology, political science, history, economics, social psychology, and even business administration.[1] As long as sociology claims to be the study of man in society, and such broad imprecision is acceptable, then educational sociology, with even less self-consciousness, will probably continue to take as its province the same wide terrain, searching enthusiastically for its special solutions. In this sense, then, educational sociology is multidisciplinary; it has never been restricted by the conventional boundaries between the social sciences.

There is an impression abroad that schools are for children and therefore not really the proper concern of sophisticated (particularly academic) adults who must grapple with the problems of the grim world. It can now be reliably reported, however, that schools spend more than 30 billion dollars annually and directly involve the lives of over 40 million people. Further reports indicate that most of the society's urgent social problems sooner or later emerge in the educational arena and that shrewd brokers in power consider the schools a good long-term investment.[2] In an increasingly technological society that needs more education for more people, there is no sign that these trends will be reversed.

It is not clear that the monitoring function of educational sociology has been fully recognized or realized. For example, in educational circles, the existence of a society outside the school is all too often little more than a rumor. This is not to claim that no one in

---

[1] The demise of the *Journal of Educational Sociology* and the subsequent creation by the American Sociological Association of the journal *Sociology of Education* illustrates the range. The new journal, after promptly rearranging the terms in the title, claims its editorial policy is eclectic; that is, it solicits contributions from all of the social sciences. Specifically named, in addition to sociology, are anthropology, economics, history, political science, and psychology. Education is not mentioned.

[2] Of course, such brokers also understand that the withholding of funds from an activity is as effective a means of manipulation as is investment in it.

either education or the society has noticed the relationships between the two spheres. It is easy to assert, however, that to the majority of people, education has tended to be an abstraction, like motherhood, which is honored but not often examined. Conversely, too many educators rarely systematically connect the events occurring outside the school with what is happening within the school. The job of the educational sociologist is to alter this cultural compartmentalization.

A job of such magnitude implies more than just a few educators invading the intellectual journals or having Bill Cosby play a schoolteacher on television. At the outset, it means having educational professionals correctly informed so that in the course of doing their jobs more effectively, *they compel social attention.* Educational sociology therefore has a training function. It must inform and interpret, but it must also train educators in the use of its information and interpretations and teach them how to incorporate its findings in their everyday decision-making. It must not only clarify social issues as they have impact on schools, it must recommend both priorities and methods in dealing with such issues. The educational sociologist would be unique in this function, since presumably only he specializes in and understands both the practical operations of schools and the real tensions of society.

Most schools avail themselves of the services of psychologists, psychiatrists, doctors, and dentists, and some even hire social workers. Few, if any, hire school sociologists. No claim of discrimination has been registered because there are not yet enough school sociologists about to muster a case. It is hoped that this condition will soon change. In the interim, some school districts seek aid from university personnel, usually sociologists from a department of sociology who are trained in the social science perspective. Academic impeccability, however, usually inhibits such sociologists from achieving very much rapport with ordinary working school people and their problems. School administrators, on the other hand, if they do not get from the sociologists the results or answers that they had predetermined they wanted, frequently employ their favorite excuse, namely, that university people do not understand the schools. Thus, the informational gap is maintained. The obvious solution is the educational sociologist, either hired by the school district as a full-time employee or at least retained as a consultant. Ideally, the educational sociologist would also be a part of the professional training team for both teachers and administrators. He would be at home in the schools as well as in the university, although he might be an organizational outcast from both. His research and insights would not only assist school districts, but they would also be fed into the preparational programs of future educational personnel. His loyalty would be to his mission rather than to an organization, which, one hopes, would result in complete objectivity and perhaps near sainthood.

I use the term *sainthood* only partly in jest. The inclination toward total resistance to change displayed by most highly organized social institutions, or even their only vaguely adequate responses to social and technological pressures for change, becomes more evident day by day. Schools and universities have achieved some of their highest accomplishments in this avoidance procedure. Anyone seeking to try to bridge the chasm between the immovable social sciences and the impenetrable schools must display remarkable forbearance, unceasing dedication, and saintly objectivity.

It is well to reiterate that discussions of education today usually mean *urban* education. Perhaps *metropolitan* would have been more precise, since *urban* may suggest to many a limiting of consideration to the central city, while *metropolitan* implies all education, city and suburban, in a given area. The point is that since some 73.5 percent (1970 census) of the people of the United States live in areas that may be classified as urban, as opposed to rural, the urban or metropolitan context is virtually implicit in our explorations of the relationships between education and society. This is not a minor consideration. I have to repeat it *sotto voce* throughout the text, since I would claim that many of the misunderstandings in today's education stem from a failure to acknowledge the implications of an urban environment.

The quality of urban life is distinctly different from that of a small town or rural settlement. The functioning of social, political, economic, and educational institutions cannot help but be shaped by the context in which these institutions exist. Education has been loath to admit this; it still dreams of the simplicity of a Mayberry, the homogeneity of Dick and Jane and *Better Homes and Gardens,* and the dispersion of strife. Schools have not yet taken seriously the urbanization of America, except perhaps as it has caused a variety of problems that are perceived as diversionary and annoying. We have been treated to a veritable torrent of literature on "inner-city" educational problems, rarely written by inner-city educators, but it has apparently washed over the schools at its highest tide and receded without much effect. The massive funds made available by Title One of the Elementary and Secondary Education Act of 1965 ("the billion-dollar misunderstanding") now seem to have had little or no impact, which suggests that the urban education literature was deficient or the schools untutored or both, assuming sincerity. It is my suspicion that both authors and educators tended to deal with symptoms rather than causes; thus reactions were essentially super-ficial. As with measles, the spots were described with remarkable accuracy; geographic location, size, shape, precise variations in hue, and intensities of itch were all documented, but without any noticeable effect upon the cause.

These problems of definition in urban education illus-trate some deeper issues for educational sociology. In the absence of a bridge between them, education and sociology have developed within traditions that are not only isolated one from the other, but also characterized by distinctly different methodologies. *Sociology* re-sides in academia; it therefore speaks in academia's language and presumes to operate within academia's methodologies, i.e., theory and empirical evidence, both arrived at through scientific proce-dures. Sociology speaks, for the most part, to itself first and then to other social scientists. It is usually unconcerned about communication with other fields, particularly applied fields such as education. *Education,* on the other hand, claims practicality over theory, action as opposed to meditation, and must speak primarily to nonprofessional, nonacademic audiences. It has been, in some part, a government activity, a business activity, a humanistic endeavor, and a semiprofessional occupation. Its relations to academia have often been those of a poor cousin.

Who listens to sociologists and who listens to educators obviously governs much of what each says and how it is said. Sociologists have not listened to educators, and educators have not listened to sociologists, but each, using his own language, has spoken, perhaps sometimes with the hope that he might at least be overheard by the other. Diplomatic relations have been sporadic, since the vested interests of each have not seemed contiguous.

To illustrate the resultant problems, let me cite sociology's concern for long-term and broad social purposes (consequences) as opposed to education's professional purposes (nonconsequential in society's eyes). Sociology may be concerned about a social institution's impact on the society, while professional education is more concerned about that institution's survival as a haven for its practitioners. This is illustrated, for example, in the tradition of educational administration that does not probe the general theory of all complex organizations, but examines only devices for the maintenance of its organization.

When you have millions of children and teachers tramping relentlessly to school each morning, day after day, week after week, month after month, it is perhaps understandable that you may be more concerned about yourself and how whatever organization you have will survive this onslaught than you are concerned about what may seem to be the luxury of exploring apparently irrelevant, complex, and even esoteric theories. In the face of this, educators have dealt with role without questioning status. Sociologists deal with status without, at least in education's case, probing role. They

11

therefore write about schools as essentially nonparticipating and distant observers, while educators read sociology as if it were a science far removed from their everyday world of work.

It should be noted that the dichotomies between education and sociology are not unique. The organization of the university into separate disciplines, each with structural detachment (separate departments, schools, or colleges), has rarely encouraged interdisciplinary communication. Similarly, the organization of schools as entities apart from other governmental functions and apart from the sequence of schooling that culminates in the university has assured a remarkable isolation from the threat of cross-fertilization. The insularity of elementary and secondary education was demonstrated when the post-Sputnik outcry for reform had little or no significant impact on the day-to-day operations of schools. The human-rights movement has had similar difficulties in penetrating the schools, except in the case of desegregation. Admittedly, the *challenge* of the human-rights movement has been potentially devastating to institutions such as education. As people frequently do when they are confronted with the need for total reappraisal, educators reacted to the challenge in panic. Some erected barricades and hoped to stem the "attack"; others ran, trying only to save some marvelously illogical piece, as people in a fire grab a bird cage or Aunt Minnie's painted china cups. These reactions were, however, consistent, for education does not have a tradition of consciously dealing with mass social movements.

It is clear that education has traditionally related best to psychology. Learning and teaching have been considered primarily individual behaviors. The treatment of phenomena in groups or classes or categories, which is the method of sociology, therefore has run counter to the tradition of education viewed psychologically. Similarly, education as an enterprise has been dominated by business perspectives through its boards of trustees largely recruited from the business and law community. Neither of these perspectives seems to encourage a sociological approach. Finally, it is interesting to note that although the educative process is frequently viewed as a cultural-transmission process, both within and without the field, there are only a handful of anthropologists active in educational matters, either on their own initiative or by request. Urbanologists frequently ignore or forget the role of schools in cities, and schools, in turn, rarely consult anyone but themselves on their problems in relating to the changing urban scene.

For a historical review of the relations between education and sociology, one can refer to W. B. Brookover's 1949 analysis[3] and then rest content that not much has changed since then except the demise of *The Journal of Educational Sociology* and a further eroding of the independence of the educationally oriented educational sociologist. It seems important to know that educational sociology as a field has been generally overwhelmed by the advocates of the sociology of education; in that development we can see why education has remained so dominated by psychology, a discipline whose adherents are not as fearful of daily contact with the educational world. When sociology "took over," education was the loser. It lost a valuable perspective, an important tool, and it lost some contact with the thinking of the social sciences on educationally related matters.

The problems of perspective, prestige, and persuasion must be acknowledged but this is not, to quote Brookover, "an elegy for educational sociology." On the contrary, recent developments in urban education, and the civil- and minority-rights fields—along with the staggering blows to public school finance, the rebellions of many young people, the Supreme Court's activities, and a host of other events—have forced the attention of many people with head-snapping suddenness back to E. G. Payne's claim for a field of study that starts with education and then uses sociology as its primary tool. The contributions of Dan Dodson, Patricia Cayo Sexton, Neal Gross,

---

[3]Wilbur B. Brookover, "Sociology of Education: A Definition," *American Sociological Review,* vol. 14, pp. 407–415, June 1949.

Abraham Bernstein, August Kerber, Barbara Bommarito, William Kvaraceus, Jean Grambs, Robert A. Dentler, and, of course, Robert Havighurst, plus a host of writers in the special field of urban education have more than adequately reinstated the perspective of educational sociology as a legitimate and much needed contribution to both the educational literature and practical sociological research in the field. We also cannot ignore the penetrating writing now emerging from the Black, Chicano, Puerto Rican, and other minority communities as they bring fresh perspectives to problems that the traditional sociology of education has forgotten, overlooked, or ignored. Finally, one must acknowledge that at least part of the reawakening of educational sociology can be attributed to those educational leaders who recognized their own need for additional data and social theory in order to deal with the pressing problems about them. Some of this leadership came from the schools themselves, some from state school officials, some from colleges and universities, some from professional organizations, and some from the U.S. Office of Education.

The educational sociologist then is a monitor and interpreter. His appraisals of both the theoretical and empirical materials of education and sociology should also enable him to forecast what may be looming on the horizon. In order to accomplish the three tasks of monitoring, interpreting, and forecasting, his training should include work in demography, social science research methodology, modern sociological theory, race and minority groups, organizational theory, community organization, social stratification, and political sociology. He might also wish to study the family, criminology, the sociology of law, and occupations. If he wishes to specialize and focus upon urban problems exclusively, he should probably be fairly well versed in urban sociology, urban politics, urban economics, and issues like welfare, housing, health care, social work, and public administration and government. The need for such breadth would seem apparent, but it may have contributed to the paucity of practitioners in the field.

Educational sociology is then a new career in education. The educational sociologist may stimulate and supervise the work of other new careerists, such as community workers, school social workers, school-community planners, and ethnic-heritage researchers. He will be a vital resource person for curriculum builders, both as a source of information and as an evaluator of the effects of the school upon the community. As schools move toward becoming metropolitan units, his demographic skills will be invaluable, just as his knowledge of the change process will be essential.

Educational sociology is alive and well; it is a rejuvenated field of study, and it expects to be doing an increasing business. In fact, it may become the most vital area in the new education in both research and application.

chapter two

education
in the city

In the beginning I must note that this will not be a complete history of the city or a review of all urban development and its complexities. In broad strokes, I propose only to accent some historical factors that seem particularly relevant to education. The only criterion is that these events relate to the people, ideas, and things that constitute schools in the urban setting.[1]

[1]Historians may protest my use of their discipline's title, feeling my approach and treatment of the data is impure history. Well and good. Perhaps they would consider then the phrase *linear sociology*, meaning a series of sociological-like observations in which the passage of time is an implicit ingredient.

My capsule version of history begins with the assertion that early America was basically a folk-rural society, mostly agricultural, and thinly populated. In 1790, only 4 percent of the population lived in urban areas. It was a society of isolated villagers, linked to an economy of family farms. Transportation was slow and tedious; communication was intermittent, often by word of mouth, frequently inaccurate, and usually slow. The two basic community institutions were the church and the school, both organized on essentially parochial lines, and often linked as a common enterprise. Legal disestablishment of religion did not destroy either institution as a central force in community life. The early American community thus tended to be a homogeneous unit, largely isolated from other units, each one organized around some common set of values, or an ecological factor, or some unique demographic structure, or perhaps some particular social compact. Identification with such communities was easy and natural, and this congregationalist arrangement became the basis of our political organization. It was *personal, intimate,* and *participatory* in the most direct town-hall sense, and reinforced by the political theories of Locke and Jefferson, aspiration toward it became an unyielding tradition, although one that was not always realized.

The less isolated, more sophisticated mercantile society along the Eastern seaboard, however, started the changes that led the nation away from its rural, small-town, handicraft, and agricultural base. Economic growth dictated the importation and utilization of European inventions that could mechanize basic American economic enterprises such as textiles, tobacco, lumber, shipbuilding, and metal products. As a raw power source, America's waterways speedily opened up the nation's industrial potential and made possible its growing participation in lucrative world trade. As the pace of commerce quickened, more rapid transportation and communication became a necessity for successful commercial competition. With the foundations of industrialization emerging, urbanization became inevitable. The establishment of manufacturing centers demanded an adequate labor supply that was both stable and in close proximity. That labor supply, in turn, demanded the provision of goods and services, also in stable quantities and readily accessible. American cities were thus born as creatures of a rapidly growing industrial society.

The two main sources of urban labor were "in-migrants" from Europe and recruits from rural America. Both groups brought with them strong identifications with earlier, smaller social and political units where control was local, personal, and easily recognized. Even though federalism was being accepted, its very name implied the continued existence of subunits with considerable autonomy. Politically, America was an alliance of sovereign states, not a unitary nation. More important, each state was an alliance of independent communities, each jealous of its identity and perceived reason for being. Kingsley Davis's classic components of a community,[2] territorial proximity and social completeness, demonstrate that kind of identity. This was not an identity that people willingly discarded. As industrialization grew, economic opportunity became more and more defined as urban-based, even for the most rural, most peasant-oriented villagers.

Industrialization and urbanization produced some other important changes. Mass production and the factory system was based upon worker specialization in a single operation of the production process. The rural generalist had to become the urban specialist. Since a strong industrial economy must continually grow in *abundance* and *diversity,* the urban worker found himself faced with an ever-expanding range of occupational specializations, each more esoteric than its predecessor, particularly as the economy diversified and became more sophisticated in its technology. Occupational specialization, in turn, produced an incredible demand for more education for more people, as our increasingly technological society does today. Then, the industrial labor movement insisted upon free public education for all so that access to the new specialties would be free. It is odd that exactly the opposite reaction

[2]Kingsley Davis, *Human Society,* Macmillan, New York, 1948, pp. 310–312.

to access seems to characterize unions today; but then, in the early days of America, they were on the outside. Now they are trying to protect what they have achieved.

Occupational specialization also led to increased interdependence, on the one hand, and a depersonalized sense of identity, on the other. As we described it elsewhere:

> Occupational specialization produced interdependence among urban people. Instead of providing for the basic essentials of living with his own hands, the urban industrial worker accepted money in exchange for his work, which he, in turn, exchanged for the goods and services which provided him with the basic necessities of life. Thus he now *buys* life. He sends his children out to be educated just as he sends out his cleaning. As a specialist, he is dependent upon the grocer for his food, the landlord for his house, the gas and electric man for his warmth. He is surrounded by strangers, and yet he is dependent upon them. His world of exchange is increasingly impersonal, and he is fearful that he can be easily exploited and forgotten. His reaction is immediate and sometimes desperate. He wants protection. He wants passage of legislation that will insure his survival by so arranging his society that his dependency cannot be exploited. And he is willing to give up some of his independence to gain such security.
>
> The urban specialist worker began to demand more ground rules to govern his relationships with the multitudes of people with whom he had to live and work in close *proximity*. He wanted policemen, firemen, building inspectors, teachers, and an abundance of laws that would insure his survival. The more complex his society became, the more numerous the alternatives of social relationships, the more he demanded rules to govern such interactions. The urban specialist worker accepted two conditions: (1) *the necessity of getting along with his fellow urbanites;* (2) *the consequent increasing community regulation of his life.*[3]

[3]Louis Fischer and Donald R. Thomas, *Social Foundations of Educational Decisions,* Wadsworth, Belmont, Calif., 1965, p. 134. With permission.

On second thought, however, the urban worker realized that he had not fully understood, or demanded, consideration of the *quality* of the urban life he had chosen. It was when he looked up from his secure workbench that he noticed that some things were missing. Thus were born what I shall call the "identity crisis" and the "quality crisis," which have come to dominate much of our folklore of the middle twentieth century.

I must pause here to make note of some other characteristics of urban growth. Cities tend in their early stages to be clusters of colonies, linked together by common plumbing. Few cities were planned in any systematic way; they just grew. For many urban residents, the city is not home; rather it is solely an economic opportunity. Many want to get away on the weekend to return to the less hurried, more spacious part of rurality, the soil, independence. In addition, urban clustering often relates to some factor of homogeneity, real or imagined, and presumably satisfies some need for the security of similarity. The security of a common language and culture tended to make new ethnic groups live near each other, for example. Workers associated with a particularly large industry also tended to cluster, for common convenience and some intangible identity of common experience. Cities then became a *confederation of neighborhoods,* inhabited by people who identified more with "their" neighborhoods than with the entire city.

Louis Wirth's classic essay "Urbanism as a Way of Life"[4] uses size, density, and heterogeneity as crucial variables in the sociological definition of a city. Size is significant because as it increases, the possibilities of a city dweller's knowing his fellow citizens on any intimate, personal basis are diminished. Superficiality, anonymity, and the transitory nature of human relations are characteristics of urban living. Impersonality, perhaps even deper-

[4]Louis Wirth, "Urbanism as a Way of Life," reprinted in Richard Sennett (ed.), *Classic Essays on the Culture of Cities,* Appleton-Century-Crofts, New York, 1969, pp. 143–164.

sonalization, begins to occur. Density tends to increase the differentiation and specialization functions, again cutting people off from each other's experience. Density also tends to encourage homogeneous populations to cluster together, even to segregate themselves or be segregated. Finally, the conglomerate city is extremely heterogeneous in social class, ethnic or racial identity, employment differentiation, age grouping, and other natural special-interest groups.

Herbert J. Gans's response to and updating of Wirth[5] does not seriously dispute Wirth's variables, but it suggests that the phenomena of the suburbs produced a second way of life in the metropolitan area. Obviously size and density decrease, and heterogeneity may or may not exist when we examine the suburbs, but it must be said that the results may be the same as in the urban center. This may occur because (1) the suburbs exist in a satellite-like relationship to the central city, meaning that the economic way of life of the city persists and dominates; (2) lacking in social completeness, the suburb never really becomes a significantly autonomous culture; and (3) heterogeneity persists, at least during the day. Incidentally, Wirth points out that the city's population since the development of suburbs is different by day, as suburbanites come to work in the city, and by night, as they leave the city and return home.

Cities also tended to grow centrifugally. It was only logical. New housing had to be built in ever-expanding rings on the edges of the city. Older housing, in the core city, was either torn down to make way for growing commercial needs or it was occupied by in-migrating poor people filling in behind the departing economically able. Often such poor were rural in origin or new citizens from other countries. The American dream of a semireturn to rurality was a larger house on a larger plot of land. As one moved up economically,

[5]Herbert J. Gans, "Urbanism and Suburbanism as Ways of Life: A Reevaluation of Definitions," in Sylvia Fleis Fava (ed.), *Urbanism in World Perspective,* Thomas Y. Crowell, New York, 1968, pp. 63–80.

a primary expression of success was the purchase of such an "estate." The older, used housing was then occupied by someone lower on the socioeconomic scale. The older and more used the area, the less desirable (frequently because of the closeness of industry and highway or railroad encroachments), the poorer the new inhabitants.

When the confederation of neighborhoods expanded, forming and re-forming into new clusters in an ever-widening circle, another phenomenon occurred. Outlying neighborhoods originally sprang up as citadels of the wealthy who had the means to remove themselves from the turmoil of the "walking city" and to detach themselves from the impersonality and growing problems of that central city. They wanted "identity," plus local control over their immediate environment, so they separated and incorporated and became suburbs, with their own schools and city governments. They were "sub-urban," meaning the presence of urbanity, but in smaller quantity, and usually incomplete, not fulfilling all of the functions of an urban center. The missing part of a suburb was usually a sustaining economic base; suburbs were largely residential. The economic base was still the central city to which one traveled each day, but from which one retreated each night. So the suburbs had different day and night populations too.

What happened with transportation might best illustrate the point that the affluent and powerful, who had isolated themselves in their own suburbs, still exercised considerable control over the urban center. Most freeway systems or rapid-transit networks are dedicated to the quick movement of suburbanites in and out of the central city. They do not serve the residents of the inner city. Quite the opposite is usually true. Freeways and rapid-transit lines often rape the environment of the inner-city dweller, either by rudely displacing him or by slashing through his community and depressing its values still further. In short, the ways in which urban transportation have developed illustrate the irony that suburban areas have sufficient power to subordinate the primary interests of the urban center to their own, to literally subsume the notion of urban welfare under the definition of the good suburban society. One part of the sickness of our cities today was contracted when the secessionist suburbs were created. It may have been the start of an entropic process that will be difficult to reverse.

Even though school districts tended to develop in the same entropic pattern as cities and suburbs, as organizations they led a separate existence. Often school-district boundaries do not comply with city boundaries. As political entities, most school districts have their own systems of control, apart in all ways from the political administration of municipal units.

This is consistent with the general history of urban areas where each special programmatic need was organized into its own autonomous political entity. Havighurst points out the incredible results of such policies when he counts over 200 separate agencies with overlapping jurisdictions in a standard metropolitan area.[6] Coordination among such agencies would require peeling off each layer to find out precisely its function and dimensions and then fitting it, like a piece of a jigsaw puzzle, into some harmonious tangency with all other agencies. Needless to say, this has not been done; it seems easier when a new need arises just to add a new layer.

The significance of this to education is (1) school districts are independent entities with little coordination with other agencies; and (2) a considerable number of other agencies that directly and obviously deal with children and educational problems have no known relationships with schools. The lack of such relationships tends to multiply the problems of people most dependent upon these governmental functions or agencies.

Meanwhile, back in the city, the sharp edges of social heterogeneity were grinding with increasing friction. Perhaps it was

[6]Robert J. Havighurst, in *Metropolitanism: Its Challenge to Education,* 67th Yearbook of the National Society for the Study of Education, The University of Chicago Press, Chicago, 1968, p. 9.

inevitable. First, it is obvious that every individual has only a selective awareness of his environment, insofar as he deals only with that environment which intrudes upon his experience. "Each man is in certain respects like all other men, like some other men, like no other man."[7] Each of our experiences is limited in some degree then by determinants such as our constitutional equipment, our group identification, the roles we play, and the special, exclusive, and wholly individual situations and events that touch us separately. Age, race, sex, geographic residence, and comparative wealth are all modifying factors. There is no simpler way to say it than Gertrude Stein's observation that "a rose is a rose is a rose."

As if that inevitable individuality were not enough, the city dweller isolated himself still further by pursuing occupational specialization to the point that few of his neighbors could identify commonality in work experience, traditionally at least one basis for communication and mutual interest and concern or both. Still further, the city offered a superabundance of stimuli that confounded absorption.

> Any metropolis can be thought of as a huge engine of communication, a device to enlarge the range and reduce the cost of individual and social choices. In the familiar telephone switchboard, the choices consist of many different lines. Plugging in the wires to connect any two lines is an act of commitment, since it implies foregoing the making of other connections . . .[8]

In short, selecting one activity meant not selecting another. Selecting commitment to one set of values precluded equal commitments to other value patterns. Since responding to all the

---

[7]Clyde Kluckhohn and Henry A. Murray, "Personality Formation: The Determinants," in *Personality in Nature, Society and Culture,* Knopf, New York, 1956, p. 53.
[8]Karl Deutch, "On Social Communication and the Metropolis," *Daedalus,* vol. 90, no. 1, Winter 1961. With permission.

possible stimuli of the city is beyond the capabilities of any individual, he must choose his "thing" or "things," and they become, for him, an identity.

That identity is associated with the values selected. Redfield defines value: "A value is a conception, explicit or implicit, distinctive of an individual or characteristic of a group, of the desirable which influences the selection from available modes, means, and ends of action."[9] Therefore, identity, that which is "distinctive of an individual" is closely associated with values, which are selected, and which select alternative behaviors. If the individual is also closely associated with a group, its values become part of both the group's identity and that of the individual member of the group. The significance of distinctive individual identity in this discussion lies in the growing influence of special-interest groups and organizations in the urban scene. In the metropolis, man, as a single voice, was lost. He selected groups and organizations as his means of expression. The number of such groups and organizations in a standard metropolitan area is almost infinite, and each is the identity (psychological as well as social and economic) of some person or persons. We call this multiplicity of such identity groups *cultural pluralism* and, again, encourage its entropic tendencies.

So, *selectively aware, selectively employed,* and *selectively committed,* we march on to increasing fragmentation and our individual Kismets, despite a simultaneous movement toward what Mumford calls "negative symbiosis,"[10] people living together in constant clash or mutual destruction of interests.

One example of such clash and destruction is racism. Deeply embedded in the ways cities developed, racism is systemic to urban culture.

[9]Robert Redfield, "Values," in S. Tax et al. (eds.), *An Appraisal of Anthropology Today,* The University of Chicago Press, Chicago, 1953, p. 97.
[10]Lewis Mumford, *The City in History,* Harcourt Brace Jovanovich, Inc., New York, 1961, pp. 571–573. With permission.

"What white Americans have never fully understood— but what the Negro can never forget—is that white society is deeply implicated in the ghetto. White institutions created it, white institutions maintain it and white society condones it."[11]

Systemic racism is racism that is a part of and an outgrowth of a social system or subsystem or what Etzioni refers to as the *organizational society.*[12] In American urban society, the existence of systemic racism is readily observable. However, its perpetuity is not necessarily inevitable, since its existence is contradictory to the ideological premises of democracy.

Much has been written about the racist attitudes, beliefs, and practices of individuals. Elaborations of various appeals to change such personal derangements have been exhaustive but, unfortunately, largely ineffective. Certainly racism is, first of all, overtly *expressed* as an individual phenomenon; Allport, Clark,[13] and a host of others have clearly recorded its pathology. However, racism's institutional or organizational roots, the capillary penetration of the basic systems and organizations of American society, have received far less attention. Some quick body blows to its points of origin are needed. I recognize the risks involved in such probings, but I shall proceed, after one brief caution.

Drawing attention to defects in a system is often construed by some as a condemnation of the entire system; for them, any adjustments or corrections suggested are ominous threats. It is not my purpose here to throw the proverbial baby out with the bath water. However, I do have to admit a strong and explicit commitment to suggest changes in this particular area.

Urban development provides some of the foundations of

[11] *Report of the National Commission on Civil Disorders,* Washington, D.C., 1968.
[12] Amitai Etzioni, *Modern Organizations,* Prentice-Hall, Englewood Cliffs, N.J., 1964, p. 1.
[13] Gordon W. Allport, *The Nature of Prejudice,* Doubleday Anchor Books, Garden City, N.Y., 1958; Kenneth B. Clark, *Prejudice and Your Child,* 2d ed., Beacon Press, Boston, 1963.

systemic racism.[14] First, the growth and power of organizations and systems is a principal characteristic of modern society.[15] Second, modern man, particularly modern urban man, in his industrial-technological setting is increasingly less independent and more interdependent, meaning he is more and more dependent upon organizations as his primary route to personal and social goal attainment.[16] Any activity or posture that tends to place any man or group of men outside the significant organizations of his society, thereby removing him from sustenance and exploiting his dependence, becomes an intention to oppress. Similarly, any act or posture within a social system and its organizations that deliberately assigns inferior status to any man or group of men because of ethnicity becomes an intention to oppress. Oppression in some form and degree is presumed to be implicit in racism.

The above premises clearly recognize Max Lerner's insistence that "access" must be the essence of American civilization[17] and that organizations have increasing control over that access. One further assertion seems in order. Control of the organizations of modern urban society generally means control of the definitions of the political, social, and economic orders of that society and perhaps its laws as well. Those excluded from access to organizational membership and power are usually forced to operate outside the definitions of the "normal" political, social, and economic orders of that society, even outside the laws derivative of

[14]I am not suggesting that racism is an exclusively urban phenomenon, either in origin or manifestation. Rural racism exists, sometimes virulently, as was witnessed in the old South. But since most Americans are urban, the problem must be solved there if it is to be solved where it has most significant impact. Racism is also more highly organized and impersonal in the city and therefore more difficult to root out or even recognize.

[15]Peter Blau and W. Richard Scott, *Formal Organizations,* Chandler, San Francisco, 1962, p. ix.

[16]Louis Fischer and Donald R. Thomas, *Social Foundations of Educational Decisions,* Wadsworth, Belmont, Calif., 1965, pp. 131–150.

[17]Max Lerner, "Humanist Goals," in Paul R. Hanna (ed.), *Education, An Instrument of National Goals,* McGraw-Hill, New York, 1962, p. 111.

those orders. It is surely a cruel irony that absolute compliance is demanded of the excluded to the laws and orders from which they have been excluded. It also seems absurd to challenge Hamilton's thesis of education's loss of "legitimacy" as a social institution for excluded people when they have had no real access to it.[18] That racism has been an integral part of the construction of the organization of American society is clearly delineated by Hofstadter, Myrdal, Laski, and other commentators.[19] That such racism was also sanctioned by law throughout our history has become patently obvious. Not so apparent, however, is the discovery that even with recent major changes in the law, as well as in its interpretations by the courts, racism still thrives; it is so interwoven in the fabric of the society that the unraveling of one legal thread seems only to lead to intersections with a dozen more, the warp and woof of which are increasingly complex and obscure. The outcome has been quite plain. There was no idealistic "melting pot" in America: it did not occur as the myth declares, and our society is still characterized by distinct and organized ethnic groupings.[20]

In spite of the repeated proclamations of belief in democracy, the system and its organizations have not yet accommodated that ideal. For visible minority groups, this digression has been particularly devastating, and even more so as they recognize that the roots of such racism are indigenous to sacred American value patterns. Those values, the values that dominated the early development of America and have been honored accordingly, now tend to leave a bitter aftertaste, mocking us because their continued application in our contemporary urban settings seems to become less and less appropriate. Specifically, an earlier America was built

[18]Charles V. Hamilton, *"Race and Education: A Search for Legitimacy,"* *Harvard Educational Review,* vol. 38, no. 4, pp. 669–684, Fall 1968.
[19]See Richard Hofstadter, *Social Darwinism in American Thought;* Gunnar Myrdal, *The American Dilemma;* and Harold J. Laski, *The American Democracy.*
[20]Nathan Glazer and Daniel Moynihan, *Beyond the Melting Pot,* M.I.T. and Harvard, Cambridge, Mass., 1963.

on such values as (1) the Puritan work-success ethic, (2) the popular rugged individualism of the frontier, and (3) the competitive ethic of nineteenth-century industrialism. In a land of seemingly unlimited resources, space, and opportunity, where inherent social Darwinism was not yet overpowering and organizations were not nearly the necessity they are today, such values were stimulants rather than depressants. But in the overorganized, overcrowded, highly educated, selectively aware, highly technological society of today, their impact tends to be reversed, particularly as they produce racism.

The work-success ethic, simply stated, is the belief that if one works and works hard enough, one is good and success will inevitably follow. Conversely, if one does not work, he is bad and does not deserve success. In an open frontier society, this belief was reinforced more often than it was denied, and few noticed that, for some ethnic groups, the society was never really open. For them, no amount of work would assure absolute success. Similarly, rugged individualism succeeded best in that expansive society where governmental intervention was minimal, where there was enough elbowroom that conflict could be avoided, and where social acceptance was a choice rather than a necessity. Urbanization and industrialization compressed living space, occupational specialization guaranteed interdependence, and the governmental role of referee became a requirement for mutual survival. Individualism was replaced by "teamwork," and Walden went public.

The competitive ethic, while not solely utilized as a social Darwinistic argument, rarely was expressed in terms other than ringing declarations of "natural selection" and "survival of the fittest." Often extolled as the ultimate national virtue, the one most likely to improve society, the competitive ethic has remained generally honored over the years, except in disclaimers by Marx and his adherents and latter-day student protest leaders. Americans have not wanted to deal with the ambiguities involved in the "competition versus democracy" argument or with the apparent contradictions of Christian ethics that are embedded in the observation that competition is not just succeeding, but succeeding at someone else's expense.[21] Certainly the essence of competition argues that gaining advantage is its primary goal. No individual or group operating under its dictates can reasonably be expected to give away advantage to any less fortunate adversary. Such "advantage" may come in social, political, economic, and even educational units, and the winners are those who can amass the most advantages.

When competitive goals are obtained solely through *individual* performance, defense of the ethic rests on naturalistic arguments, for example, the notion that competition is unassailable because rivalry between individuals is a universal human condition. This is not true, of course. Competition between individuals is an unknown concept in some cultures; therefore it is obviously not a natural state of man. Whether competition between groups of men is natural is not yet decided.[22] When *organizations* take over, controlling what will be contested and who will be allowed access to the contests, the competitive ethic, applied to either individuals or groups, is even less defensible. In such a context, there is little left but oppression for those who have been excluded. It is clear then that the popular slogan of "working within the system" is more than just an alternative strategy; it is a literal passport to participation and survival.[23] To reiterate, any activity or posture that tends to place any

[21]"Rivalry for the purpose of obtaining some advantage over some other person or group," *American College Dictionary,* Random House, New York, 1947.

[22]The arguments about man's tribalism and whether or not he is responsive to the territorial imperative are still not empirically verified, but as speculation, they are intriguing.

[23]I am not overlooking Durkheim's argument that competition promotes differentiation (division of labor). Obviously, if individuals cannot *survive* in existing areas of competition, they may create new roles and functions in which they can succeed. But those roles and functions may have to be outside the system, if the system is racist and exclusionary and capable of co-opting the new activity. Whites may find it altogether impossible to compete and dominate an activity in which the prerequisites are minority racial membership and enculturation.

man or group outside the significant organizations of their society, thereby preventing access to the competition, removes such persons from sustenance and exploits their dependence. This constitutes an intention to oppress, because any success or advantage obtained at the expense of the already disadvantaged or excluded can only be oppression.

The competitive ethic is as implicit in American urban culture as is systemic racism, and in most destructive aspects, it has been one of the major producers and sustainers of that racism. Even the way in which we speak about our organizational society, i.e., the *cui bono* (Who benefits?) classification system of organizations,[24] reflects the pragmatic recognition that organizations, when penetrated to their bedrock *raison d'être,* are essentially self-serving and competitive. It has apparently been perceived that holding racist and competitive values is more advantageous to an organization than it is disadvantageous, for the significant and dominant organizations of American urban society have been, for the most part, implicitly racist and competitive. One obvious reason is that racial exclusion policies decrease the range of competition and thereby serve the selected self-interests of the excluders. Such exclusion is often justified by claims of "freedom of choice" and, of course, the equal opportunity for reciprocity of exclusion. If the rich exclude the poor from their lives, the poor have a right to exclude the rich; or if the well-fed exclude the hungry, the hungry may exclude the well-fed from their hunger. The real issue is what one is being excluded from, and the answer can suggest such gross inequities in reciprocal exclusion that the whole question becomes a cruel and abusive jest.[25]

[24]Blau and Scott, op. cit., p. 42.
[25]An underlying theme of anger and violence in the competitive ethic is revealed in such common expressions as "wipe out the opposition" and "kill off the competition." Such expressions were acted out with great brutality in efforts, for example, to stop the labor movement in its formative years; this is being repeated now against black activities that automatically exclude whites.

Even so, dominant organizations today add insult to injury when they angrily scream "foul" at excluded people who do attempt to reciprocate exclusion by claiming the right and the desire to exclude advantaged groups from their lives. The outcry against "black separatism" is one prime example. It is argued that black separation would be unhealthy for the nation and perhaps even destructive to the fabric of democracy. While this may be true, if blacks have already been excluded from the real competition, which they have been to all intents and purposes, it is difficult to see how codifying that exclusion could change things except perhaps to give blacks an arena in which they could successfully compete and evade white domination. It is true that the threat of codifying exclusion would compel attention to the contradictions in the democratic ideal and would demand a clear answer to the value question involved. However, that kind of discussion would seem to be healthy and constructive.[26]

As our urban, highly organized society has become more complex and sophisticated, the locus of the power that can grant or deny access has become less and less obvious. Certainly it does not necessarily rest in the public sector, even though in the democratic context that is where such key decisions are supposed to be made. Actually, those who make decisions on access or exclusion issues may now be so camouflaged by intricate organizations and, as in the case of suburbanites, by geography as well that outgroups cannot readily identify correct targets for their petitions or dissent. Even men of good will, seeking to implement democracy and abolish exclusion, have difficulty distinguishing the issues. Thomas Wolfe wrote eloquently on some aspects of their dilemma.

> I think the enemy comes to us with the face of innocence—with false words and lying phrases, saying: See I am one of you—I

---

[26]Avoidance of the issue is, however, more prevalent, perhaps because "the exaltation of winning dampens any moral feelings you have" (Martin Erdmann, *Life Magazine,* Mar. 12, 1971).

am one of your children, your son, your brother, and your friend. Behold how sleek and fat I have become—and all because I am just one of you, and your friend. Behold how rich and powerful I am—and all because I am one of you—shaped in your way of life, of thinking, of accomplishment. What I am, I am because I am one of you, your humble brother and your friend. Behold, cries Enemy, the man I am, the man I have become, the thing I have accomplished—and reflect. Will you destroy this thing? I assure you that it is the most precious thing you have. It is yourselves, the projection of each of you, the triumph of your individual lives, the thing that is rooted in your blood, and native to your stock, and inherent in the traditions of America. It is the thing that all of you may hope to be, says Enemy, for humbly, am I not just one of you? Am I not just your brother and your son? Am I not the living image of what each of you may hope to be, would wish to be, would desire for his own son? Would you destroy this glorious incarnation of yourselves—you kill the thing that is most gloriously American, and in so killing, kill yourselves.[27]

It is easy to see, too, that Wolfe's Enemy now comes to speak to us with instant and total communications at his command. Via the communications explosion, we offer more of everything and more kinds of things, good and bad, pure or polluted, than has any other culture at any time in the world's history. With electronic technology, we daily experience a communications overkill that leaves our senses bewildered. McLuhan has claimed dramatically that our children must interrupt their education to go to school, which, freely translated, means that modern communications are so total and exciting that children find school dull in contrast. In the multistimuli urban environment, such communications finally become too much, numbing the senses and making identity the margin of sanity.

Our most prominent urbanologist, Lewis Mumford, sees

[27]Excerpt from pp. 742–743 from *You Can't Go Home Again* by Thomas Wolfe. Copyright 1934, 1937, 1938, 1939, 1940 by Maxwell Perkins as Executor. By permission of Harper & Row, Publishers, Inc.

the American city as being at some kind of crossroads. To the right is continuing urban expansion in the service of economic and power goals to the distress of whatever humanism we still possess. To the left is an uncharted way that directs us to try anew.

> The chief function of the city is to convert power into form, energy into culture, dead matter into living symbols of art, biological reproduction into social creativity. The positive functions of the city cannot be performed without creating new institutional arrangements, capable of coping with the vast energies modern man now commands: arrangements just as bold as those that originally transformed the overgrown village and its stronghold into the nucleated, highly organized city.[28]

Mumford goes on to say:

> Before modern man can gain control over the forces that now threaten his very existence, he must resume possession of himself. This sets the chief mission for the city of the future: that of creating a visible regional and core structure, designed to make man at home with his deeper self and his larger world, attached to images of human nurture and love.[29]

The ideal city then would have some distinctive characteristics: (1) it would be limited in size so that it could not tyrannize its population; (2) it would maintain its precious relationship with the open countryside surrounding it; (3) its land would be publicly controlled to assure use for maximum public welfare; (4) it would enslave technology, including the automobile, rather than be enslaved; and (5) it would be both a museum and laboratory for human development.

[28]Lewis Mumford, *The City in History*, Harcourt Brace Jovanovich, Inc., New York, 1961, p. 571. With permission.
[29]Ibid., p. 573. With permission.

Mumford also sees education as being the center of activities, evidently because education is the logical activity of human development. He does not refer to "schooling," which may be interpreted as neither an endorsement nor a rejection of schools, but rather as possibly an acceptance of the notion that schooling is only one form among many forms of education.

Mumford's ideal city is not a sprawling metropolis with its social institutions such as the school laid out in prostrated complexity. Participation is a key concept, as are ecological balance and the ability to maintain possession of oneself. Mumford says:

> The final mission of the city is to further man's conscious participation in the cosmic and the historic process. Through its own complex and enduring structure, the city vastly augments man's ability to interpret these processes and take an active, formative part in them, so that every phase of the drama it stages shall have, to the highest degree possible, the illumination of consciousness, the stamp of purpose, the color of love. That magnification of all the dimensions of life, through emotional communion, rational communication, has been the supreme office of the city in history. And it remains the chief reason for the city's continued existence.[30]

There are those who find Mumford's ideal in the Newtown concept,[31] although the homogeneity of such communities and their domination by corporations for profit make such a claim suspect. What is clear to the educator is, of course, that he must play a vital role in the future city. Someone has said that "a city cannot rise above its school system." If this is true, then indeed the society needs to get about the business of rebuilding its schools.

[30]Ibid., p. 576. With permission.
[31]See, for example, the communities of Columbia, Maryland, and Reston, Virginia. An alternative look at new cities can be found in Walter McQuade (ed.), *Cities Fit to Live In,* Macmillan, New York, 1971.

In discussing those characteristics of urban America with which we are most concerned because of their implications for education, I started with the notion that people wanted personal, intimate, and direct participatory government because it was one way to maintain personal identity. The onslaught of abundance and diversity created by a young, expansive, vigorously competitive economy produced urbanization and occupational specialization, both of which undermined that identity. Urbanization crowded and compressed people; occupational specialization spawned their interdependence; and their interdependence provoked demands for increasing governmental regulation of overtaxed social relationships. For many, the city was not home; home was, at worst, a neighborhood, at best, someplace elsewhere, less complicated and overpowering. Cities were really confederations of neighborhoods, some of which, on the outer edges, broke off and became separate entities called suburbs. Such suburbs were often more affluent and were the area of residence of the wealthy and politically powerful decision makers who directed the destinies of the central city, but most often with greater concern for the welfare of their suburbs than for the welfare of the urban center.

The problem of overstimulation in the city, particularly as caused by mass communications, was also considered. I concluded that it was inevitable, in the face of such conditions, that the urban dweller had to be selectively aware, selectively responsive, and selectively committed to values, organized interest groups, and his own special vision in order to survive. For some, this meant oppressing others, and I pointed to racism as a primary mechanism for exclusion and oppression if used with sufficient frequency, particularly by key organizations and decision makers. I said racism had become systemic and difficult to root out of the fabric of urban culture because it was reinforced by the persuasive competitive ethic that was credited with producing our highest achievements; and because the generating power behind racism could so easily hide in a culturally pluralistic society that at least rhetorically applauded differences and celebrated their maintenance. Finally, I called upon Thomas Wolfe and Lewis Mumford to give us two different perspectives and perhaps point a way to the future.

Two questions come to mind when we turn to examine public education as it exists in the urban environment that has just been described. The first is: Can the schools still survive in the field of education? And the second is an appropriate reversal of George Count's famous question of 1932: Dare the social order of today build new schools? American public education grew to maturity primarily as the vision of the essentially rural, small-town, and suburban white middle classes for whom education had become the key to vertical mobility and economic privilege. Accordingly, organized education has always been characterized as economical, possibly even frugal, static, in the sense that it acted as a cultural-maintenance agent, and singular and didactic about its purpose of producing one *cultural ideal.* Earlier the school was proclaimed as the great assimilator of diverse cultural groups, but we now realize that such a claim was premature and maybe downright false, except insofar as it may have reflected a hope.

In fact, the schools attempted to design themselves after the efficiency models of corporate agriculture and industry, single-product systems engineered to produce a better ear of corn, a larger chicken, a nicer washing machine, or a faster car. In the schools, the system was supposed to operate to hammer differences into like-nesses and produce an ideal model, which turned out to be someone who could step into the professional or corporate middle-class lifestyle. Such a model was epitomized in the lives of the children found in elementary school readers, the enculturation model in-troduced in most public schools.

Dick and Jane are two Anglo-Saxon children who live with their middle-class father and mother, a baby brother/sister, and a dog named Spot/Perky in a suburban, detached, well-mortgaged, single-family dwelling with well-kept lawns dotted with trees and toys, in a neighborhood of similar homes, all interchangeable with

37

spare parts available at nearby shopping centers. Fortunately, Dick and Jane have a jovial grandfather and grandmother who live not far away on the most remarkably diversified family farm, ranch, and Frontierland known to the world. The children each have separate bedrooms, nice, clean, and fashionable clothes, plenty of food, an abundance of toys, and likable friends. All of the children have exceptionally good manners, rarely ever pout, and seem to control their environment with the ease of Harold and his Purple Crayon. And, like Orphan Annie, they never seem to grow up.

Father goes to work each day in a suit and tie and seems to be extremely friendly and handy about the house on weekends. His corporation salary provides well, and he does not get in the way. Mother, on the other hand, is an accomplished cook, housekeeper, seamstress, and child psychologist, as well as an all-inclusive figure of goodness who smells like hot buttered toast. She is obviously not an advocate of Women's Liberation. The family plays together, goes to some indistinguishable church together, and goes on vacations together. Obviously it stays together without strife or divorce or financial stress. Life is a rosy place inhabited by friendly community helpers, such as friendly policemen, friendly milkmen, and friendly neighbors who live on Cherry Street. In short, Dick and Jane are a product, produced according to specifications largely dictated by corporate production-model thinking.

Once educators set up such a model, they then tried to set up standards and procedures and an organization that would guarantee production of replicas of the model. The outcome was to define the process. How the children and the teachers would be organized, how the curriculum would be organized, and even how the buildings would be organized were all to be an outgrowth of the model. The meaning of key educational terms, themselves vital to the definition of the educational process, was similarly restricted to reinforcing the model. Words like *intelligence, achievement, school success,* and *personal goodness* were held up to the model, which set the standard against which all things were measured. Rewards, punishments, promotions, professional achievement of teachers, and administrative skill, all were compared to the Dick and Jane standard, and appropriately so, considering the goal.

If we create a factory to produce Ford automobiles, we thereby define our needs for raw materials, for processed parts, and for final assembly *in terms of the product.* Every worker up and down the line is organized in such a way that he knows precisely what his job is in the process that produces Ford automobiles. Any modifications introduced into the production process are to increase efficiency, not to divert the system from its purpose of producing the desired automobiles. If, at the end of the assembly line, a renegade lawn mower or bathtub were to appear, there would be panic. A frantic search would be instituted to find out what went wrong, what part of the system failed. No one would have a moment's peace until the error had been rooted out.[32]

So it has been with the single-product-model school. So too have we defined what may be the essence of the problems of urban education. Gathered up and tied in a package, the problems of urban education are decorated with words like *relevance, quality, bureaucracy, disadvantage, desegregation, alienation, unrest,* and *community participation.* Reduced still further to the point of near oversimplification, we are talking about what happens in a modern, wildly pluralistic society when a child socialized in total or in part in a one-family-neighborhood-cultural group system confronts a vast urban school system that is operating on different premises of time-relevance and model-relevance. Because of these differences, the school is acculturating, but it thinks and proceeds as if it were enculturating. The code words tell the story.

relevance   Not long ago, a child in school raised the question:

---

[32]It is clear that there are some educators who yearn for the old days of the Model T with its single black decor, but even they do not argue about the appropriateness of producing cars.

"What has all this got to do with me and my world?" Leaving out the antihistorical biases of all younger generations, the question points to a system that has become fixed in form and structure and needs to adjust from its past-relevance to a present-relevance, from its single model (to which fewer and fewer youngsters can relate, even Dick and Jane) to the multiple models that the multiple stimuli in the environment demand.

quality   Defined as value on a continuum, the current standard of excellence remains that which best produces the professional lifestyle. Achievement is defined in terms of the learner's accomplishing system-defined tasks that are associated with, for example, high verbal facility, middle- or upper-class perceptions and experiences, and abstract thinking of the kind that is related to system-approved occupations and carried on in system-approved language.

bureaucracy   The frustrations with complex organizations and the impersonality in education that have made bureaucracy a pejorative term are associated with the unyielding posture of educational form and structure when confronted with new developments, social change, or a diversity of clients. That schools are not bureaucracies in any classical sense is still another issue.

disadvantage   This is a kind term used to mean children who differ from the single model. Explicitly, the term states that anyone different (particularly racially or economically) is at a disadvantage when confronting the narrow range approved of or likely to succeed in schools. Compensatory education is that activity which seeks to change the different child into a replica of the model and assumes that his differences are disadvantages, even deficiencies, that need to be compensated for so that he can become "normal."

desegregation   Desegregation is a democratic dream, which, when it is talked of in the educational context, most often means making black or other minority children into white children by mixing them with white children. There is little doubt that sincere educators clearly recognize that segregation (or stigmatization) is harmful to children, but their solution, making minority kids into carbon copies of the single model, is perhaps more harmful in the long run.

alienation   Melvin Seeman's five dimensions of alienation[33] spell out the results of the present urban educational system's dysfunctionalism.

1   *Powerlessness*   The expectancy or probability held by the individual student that his own behavior cannot determine the occurrence of the outcomes, or reinforcements, he seeks.

2   *Norm-conflict*   The perception on the part of the individual student that his personal norms are in conflict with those of the school organization of which he is a member.

3   *Uncertainty*   Low expectancy on the part of the individual student that satisfactory predictions about future outcomes of behavior can be made.

4   *Isolation*   A feeling on the part of the individual student of separation from the school organization, or isolation from its standards.

5   *Self-estrangement*   A perception on the part of the individual student that school organizational goals and standards have been substituted for his own.

It is clear that more and more children and youths exhibit increasing alienation from the schools just as many adults now

[33]Melvin Seeman, "On the Meaning of Alienation," *American Sociological Review,* vol. 24, pp. 782–783, October 1959.

recognize their alienation from the corporate society. High dropout rates, drug addiction, and radical antiestablishment activities are just some more extreme examples of students "tuning out," of being alienated.

unrest Increasing alienation obviously produces increasing unrest, aimlessness, antiorganization defiances, and hostility in varying degrees and kinds.

community participation The present demand for more community participation is a restatement of the now classic desire of Americans to rule their own institutions personally, intimately, and directly. Clearly a response to the perceived detachment of schools from reality and the resulting alienation, community participation is a search for lost identity.

Merton, the sociologist, states my principal thesis in a different (more academic) way when he says:

> No society lacks norms governing conduct. But societies do differ in the degree to which the folkways, mores and institutional controls are effectively integrated with the goals which stand high in the hierarchy of cultural values. The culture may be such as to lead individuals to center their emotional connections upon the complex of culturally acclaimed ends, with far less emotional support for prescribed methods of reaching out for these ends. With such differential emphasis upon goals and institutional procedures, the latter may be so vitiated by the stress on goals as to have the behavior of many individuals limited only by considerations of technical expediency . . . As this process of attenuation continues, the society becomes unstable and there develops what Durkheim called "anomie" (or normlessness).[34]

[34]Robert Merton, *Social Theory and Social Structure,* Free Press, New York, 1957, pp. 135–136. With permission.

And Erich Fromm stresses my point about the competitive system.

> It needs men who cooperate smoothly in large groups; who want to consume more and more, and whose tastes are standardized and can be easily influenced and anticipated. It needs men who feel free and independent, who do not feel subject to any authority or principle or conscience, yet are willing to be commanded, to do what is expected, to fit into the social machine without friction—men who can be guided without force, led without leaders, be prompted without any aim except the one to be on the move, to function, to go ahead. Modern capitalism has succeeded in producing this kind of man; he is the automaton, the alienated man. He is alienated in the sense that his acts and forces become estranged from him; they stand above and against him, and rule him rather than being ruled by him.[35]

Thus the educational system's dysfunctionalism today is an outcome of several sociohistorical developments that seem to manifest themselves with greater virulence in urban areas. As the composition of the population of the inner city changed, it became an alien population in terms of the single-model system. Any place where there are "outsiders" (nonmodel groups) and "insiders" (model groups) contains the appropriate conditions for dysfunctionalism. Dysfunctionalism, of course, may differ in degree and kind since it is a function both of the *intensity* of the social-exclusion mechanisms directed against the aliens and of the *differences* between the target groups of systemic violence and the model groups. Educational dysfunctionalism is rarely an exclusive condition; it reflects the tensions and pressure of society, particularly

[35]Erich Fromm, "The Present Human Condition," in Hendrick M. Ruitenbeck (ed.), *Varieties of Modern Social Theory,* Dutton, New York, 1963, pp. 73–74. With permission.

in its resistance to change and to adaptation to new conditions.

It is conceivable that such resistance has had two results: First, it has diverted education from its original purpose; and second, it inadvertently becomes an accomplice in activities that it usually denounces. Margaret Mead points out the first result when she says:

> [American] education has been enormously influenced by the articulate need to assimilate the masses of European immigrants, with the resultant phrasing of the public schools as a means for educating other people's children. The schools ceased to be chiefly a device by which accumulated knowledge or skills were taught to children and became a practical device for arousing and maintaining national loyalty through inculcating a language and a system of ideas which pupils did not share with their parents. . . . [The system where] the other human beings are conceived of as inferior to those who are making the plans has been a boomerang which has destroyed our whole educational philosophy; it has shifted the emphasis from one of growth and seeking for knowledge to one of dictation and forced acceptance of cliches and points of view.[36]

In the second case, it is clear that the dictatorial and suppressive actions of the single-product-model school system may be stimulating and sustaining radical and racial militancy. The radical strategy may well be to encourage perpetuation of educational dysfunctionalism in order to "radicalize" racial minorities and other "outgroups," with the notion that eventually an alliance of such forces will topple the entire social structure as we now know it.

Change in schools must be initiated by both the society and the school system and then implemented by the professional

---

[36]Margaret Mead, "Our Educational Emphasis in Primitive Perspective," *American Journal of Sociology,* vol. 48, pp. 633–639, 1943. With permission.

educators. The social order must build new schools that will reflect what the social order wishes to do to respond to changing conditions and the problems they educe, particularly in the city. In some measure, education's own theoretical development ultimately waits for that direction, or as William O. Stanley states it:

> Every aspect of the educational enterprise implies some theory of education, as every theory of education implies some conception of the nature of man, of the meaning of the good and public welfare, of the nature of knowledge and the way in which it is discovered and tested, of the relation of the school to the social order, including the process of change, of the basis of authority in education and the way in which man should be related to man in the cooperative and associative enterprise of human life. Further, every suggestion for change or reorganization in the conduct of the schools, in greater or lesser degrees is dogged by these theoretical implications. The theoretical components of the educational enterprise are there whether we are aware of them or not.[37]

Such key questions, which neither the social order nor the schools have yet resolved, or even acknowledged in some cases, are fundamental value questions. Racism is not an academic question; it is a moral issue that arouses high feelings. Student unrest, even though presently a symptom, not a cause, similarly causes high-decibel discussions. Opposition to the Establishment, almost always perceived as irrational by some (rightfully, in some instances), is met with swift and sure resistance and open hostility, and in some cases, the powerful decision makers blindly lash out at it with all the subtlety of a rural Mississippi sheriff at a black-militant rally.

[37]William O. Stanley, "The Social Foundations Subjects in the Professional Education of Teachers," *Educational Theory*, vol. 18, no. 3, pp. 224–236, Summer 1968. With permission.

It is hardly necessary to argue that education rests on considerations of value and principles of conduct. Every educational
system embodies characteristic social aims and appraisals of
practice, distinctive attitudes toward character, and conceptions of a desirable human life. It is no cause for wonder, then,
that educational issues engage the moral passions.[38]

In the context of Mumford's urban "negative symbiosis,"
and in the presence of many heated affective debates, the stability of
the traditional single-model-product system may seem to some like a
welcome port in a storm. However, such a snug harbor is deceiving;
its existence, in reality, is only contributing more energy to the storm.
Educators, huddled below decks, have been either unaware of or
unwilling to confront their central role and have insisted that society
present them with hand-stitched, appropriate, clear-cut directions.
True, education as a central experience could be the arena in which
the new social order sorts out its conflicts and confusions and finds
its way into the future. Mumford envisions that role in the ideal city of
the future when he says:

Not industry but *education* will be the center of . . . activities;
and every process and function will be evaluated and approved
just to the extent that it furthers human development, whilst the
city itself provides a vivid theater for the spontaneous encounters and challenges and embraces of daily life.[39]

I suspect that education in urban America will need to
confront major social policy issues and redefine its own responses in
terms of the resolution of those issues. That probably means reorganization from tip to toe, it is hoped with two injunctions constantly
in mind. First, education, for most people in America, takes place in

[38]Israel Scheffler, in Preface to R. S. Peter, *Ethics and Education,* Scott,
Foresman, Chicago, 1967.
[39]Mumford, *The City in History,* p. 573. With permission.

an urban environment and such an environment, when fully examined, offers both a set of constraints and a myriad of challenges and opportunities. Second, education needs to attend to Frank Lloyd Wright's dictum that "form should follow function." The use of intelligence should also be considered. I also suspect that education needs to inform its patrons honestly and forthrightly that it is experiencing a multiracial, multicultural, multistimuli urban environment that tends to dehumanize and depersonalize the educative process. Education has extreme difficulty operating effectively in such a context, given its outmoded and never efficient single-model system, its financial anemia, and the tumult of debates raging in and out of its domain.

chapter three

the importance of being equal

The Declaration of Independence states that all men are created equal. This was clearly meant as a political assertion; it did not apply to the economic, social, and psychophysical realms. If acted upon, it means that, to use Max Lerner's words, everyone is supposed to have the same "access" to the opportunity to full and free participation in the society, even in the various arenas where equality is not a guarantee. In contrast, the economic world of competitive capitalism has always assumed an inherent and valued inequality among its participants. Similarly, the social-stratification system present in most organized societies in the world confirms an expected social inequality. Of course, the presence of individual differences in physical constitution and psyche seems to guarantee differences there too. These latter differences are functions of the individual's socialization process, his natural selective perception and awareness, and his hereditary constitutional determinants, all of which are too persuasive to deny. The results are clear; we are a heterogeneous nation in all ways, except perhaps as we have attempted a long standing and revolutionary commitment to be homogeneous in matters of political and civil rights.

In many ways, this has been a messy and confusing arrangement. It is difficult to have political equality (or maintain it) without yearnings and expectations for social and economic equality too. The reality of natural individual differences only contributes further to the many curious and uncomfortable relationships our system has devised. America is faced with a problem of cultural flow. How do you keep the system chugging along when there are so many disparities among the various subsystems and subgroups, held together now with only a legendary democratic framework?

Historically, the job of overcoming the confusions and contradictions of the system was, at least in part, assigned to education. Education, said Horace Mann, "beyond all other devices of human origin" was "the great equalizer of the conditions of men, the balance wheel of the social machinery."[1] But the concept of equality, as it was applied in both principle and practice in education, was always a tentative commitment, with the result that we are prone to observe that in American education equal educational opportunity has rarely been achieved. Part of the difficulty lies in defining the concepts *equal* (in education) *educational* and *opportunity* (in education) as they are encountered in the context of our political democracy, but also in our capitalistic economic system, our socially stratified society, and our heterogeneous background of cultures, races, and natural individual differences, all of which are in a state of constant change in time and circumstance.

[1]Horace Mann, quoted in Merle Curti, *The Social Ideas of American Educators,* rev., Littlefield, Adams, Paterson, N.J., 1959, p. 122.

Using Peter Rose's typology, American education has confronted the fact of its heterogeneity with at least three models: Assimilation, amalgamation, and cultural pluralism.[2] *Assimilation* requires conformity to a single model, which was originally defined by largely traditional British political, social, cultural, and religious institutions. Expressed in school terms, it is the Dick and Jane culture. *Amalgamation* was based on a vision of a new American culture emerging from the best elements of many cultural inputs. It was the melting-pot notion of the superior alloy. Since it was never clear just who was in charge of selecting the degree and kind of elements for the alloy, assimilation's Anglo single model became, like Orwell's pig, "more equal than others."[3] The model of *cultural pluralism* grew from ideas of strength in diversity, a "multiplicity in a unity, an orchestration of mankind, with, of course, equality and justice for all, a humane and tolerant society."[4]

The etiology of the currently recognized dysfunctional-ism of education, particularly in urban areas, suggests the failure of the assimilation model. In fact, the increasing awareness of the magnitude of the problem of unassimilated students in our schools may be the motivation for the current recognition that in reality the amalgamation model was also largely legendary, a myth, a dream unfulfilled. Silberman has remarked: "To be sure, these groups have been transformed by several generations of life in America; . . . yet the ethnic groups are not just a political anachronism; they are a reality. [Even] integration did not mean assimilation . . ."[5]

[2]Peter I. Rose, *They and We,* Random House, New York, 1964, pp. 49–57.
[3]George Orwell, *Animal Farm,* Harcourt, Brace, New York, 1946, p. 112.
[4]Horace M. Kallen, "Democracy Versus the Melting-Pot," *The Nation,* vol. 100, pp. 190–194, February 18, 1915. With permission. Copyright © by Horace Kallen.
[5]Charles E. Silberman, *Crisis in Black and White,* Random House, New York, 1964, p. 165. See also Nathan Glazer and Daniel Moynihan, *Beyond the Melting Pot,* M.I.T. and Harvard, Cambridge, Mass., 1963.

But heterogeneity persists, just as, and perhaps because, the notion of political freedom persists. Deliberate policies to "de-culture" ethnic groups, to cleanse them of their ethnicity, have consistently failed, even though it is clear that such policies have taken their toll among such groups in degradation and even outright oppression. On the other hand, it is obvious that there is a system of social stratification in American society that categorizes people using both economic and ethnic criteria. The net result has been to maintain the assumptions of superiority inherent in the British-oriented assimilation model, thereby maintaining its social, economic, and political power. Culture, states Francis E. Merrill:

> (1) . . . is the characteristically human product of social interaction; (2) it provides socially acceptable patterns for meeting biological and social needs; (3) it is cumulative as it is handed down from generation to generation in a given society; (4) it is meaningful to human beings because of its symbolic quality; (5) it is learned by each person in the course of his development in a particular society; (6) it is, therefore, a basic determinant of personality; and (7) it depends for its existence upon the continued functioning of the society but it is independent of any individual or group.[6]

A subculture, on the other hand, may be defined as:

> A group within the main culture which displays in its organized or patterned behavior some elements which differentiate it from the main cultural pattern sufficiently to be recognized as a special sub-group.[7]

It is clear by these definitions that there are few pure

[6]Francis E. Merrill, *Society and Culture: An Introduction to Sociology,* 2d ed., Prentice-Hall, Englewood Cliffs, N.J., 1961, p. 116. With permission.
[7]Louis Fischer and Donald R. Thomas, *Social Foundations of Educational Decisions,* Wadsworth, Belmont, Calif., 1965, p. 26. With permission.

cultures existing in the United States that stand apart as distinct from the dominant culture patterns that evolved from years of attempts at assimilation and amalgamation. America then has a dominant cultural thrust; it is the British-oriented assimilation model, but it has been modified to a degree by the sheer necessity of accommodating in some measure a wide variety of other culture patterns. No one has selected the best in any conscious decision-making process. People have just adjusted to survive; they have tolerated differences, often unwillingly, but nevertheless, they have permitted differences. What has developed is an uneasy truce, an irregular cultural flow of sorts, but one that is often highly explosive as groups compete with one another for power and social and economic supremacy. Nothing in American educational history seems to indicate any real recognition of cultural pluralism, or even subcultural pluralism. The clamor of the civil-rights movement, however, has recently awakened American education to the fact that it has been systematically excluding significant groups of people. Education's first response to this new vision of society was to admit exclusion, but, at the same time, to defensively structure its response in such a way that the excluded were blamed for being "different" or "deprived of the dominant culture."

Thus, with "compensatory" education anyone different (particularly racially or economically) was in need of special attention that would remove those disadvantageous differences and make him more like the model (Dick and Jane). The results are obvious. The Elementary and Secondary Education Act's Title I program for compensatory education is now called the "billion-dollar misunderstanding" because it sought to acculturate all subcultures by using enculturation methods and because it never doubted the appropriateness of the single assimilation model. Compensatory education simply did not work. It may even have made matters worse as subcultures dug in their heels and resisted, even to the point of violence and total alienation.

Sociologist David Rogers remarks that writers on both

the right and the left now agree that "public education, an institution that was established for egalitarian and democratic reasons, has now turned into an instrument that perpetuates inequality."[8] It is also true, however, that we have not defined *equality.* It is easy to observe that equality is in some ways like wealth; it may be difficult to define, but you are terribly sure about its absence. One thing is certain, equality is not sameness. Human beings, as political, social, economic, and intellectual animals, are not the same, and it seems highly unlikely that they ever will be or, more importantly, ever want to be. Every man does, however, want to be something; he is what he feels himself to be; he has some goal. Equality, expressed as educational opportunity, must then be a process that allows each man the opportunity to develop himself to the full in whatever direction he chooses as long as that path does not violate the equality of others. Certainly the educational process should neither rob any man of his identity nor disparage that identity nor presume to either limit or direct his aspirations.

Segregation violates the identity of those segregated. The United States Supreme Court's 1954 decision quite specifically referred to this concept when it said: "to separate them from others of similar age and qualifications solely because of their race generates a feeling of inferiority as to their status in the community that may affect their hearts and minds in a way unlikely ever to be undone."[9] Similarly, the Dick and Jane single-product model clearly violates the options of those whose aspirations may stray from the paths of righteousness leading to the professional lifestyle. The single-product model, introduced by some as an answer to equality in that they thought that offering the *same* curriculum would be equivalent to equality of opportunity, robs the non-English speaker of his identity, the immigrant of his heritage, and the racial minority child of his rights.

[8]David Rogers, *110 Livingston Street,* Random House, New York, 1968, p. 486.
[9]*Brown et al. v. Board of Education of Topeka et al.,* 347 U.S. 483 (1953).

Coleman rightfully points out that the notion of the "common" curriculum is faulty because "it accepts as given the child's expected future."[10] In other words, it fixed him early in his place in future society. The single model acts to sort out those who conform from those who do not conform according to the sole standard of performance implied in the model. Talcott Parsons verifies this when he observes: "It is therefore not stretching the evidence too far to say broadly that the primary selective process occurs through differential school performance in elementary school, and that the seal is put on it in junior high school."[11]

The United States Supreme Court's desegregation decision, however, introduced a new assumption. The Court was now concerned with results, with the effects of the schooling process. It was not enough to say that you started children on an equal basis (not that this had ever been done) if they ended up unequal. Since inequality was unnatural, there had to be something in the process that had gone wrong. Separation, claimed to be equal at least at the start (it was not), was declared inherently unequal because it imposed a set of conditions upon the educational process that could only produce unequal results.

The Court was also defining as civil rights social arrangements as old as the nation itself. It was declaring social stratification and differentiation based upon race as legally (politically) unacceptable. Even more recently, lower courts in California and Texas (and there are similar suits in courts in many other states) have ruled that a state may not allow unequal tax resources to prevent any child's access to equal educational opportunity. Not only have the courts entered the social and political arenas to try and remove causes of inequality, but they have also entered the economic arena. It is not yet known whether anyone will file suit to

[10]James Coleman, "The Concept of Equality of Educational Opportunity," *Harvard Educational Review,* vol. 38, no. 1, p. 13, Winter 1968. With permission.

[11]Talcott Parsons, "The School Class as a Social System," *Harvard Educational Review,* vol. 29, no. 2, p. 299, Fall 1959.

achieve intellectual equality, although it is rumored that some behaviorists are discussing the matter. It is abundantly clear that to deal with the issues surrounding equality, social and economic justice, and the attainment of a truly equalitarian society, we must encounter as many viewpoints and emotions as there are writers, lecturers, proclaimers, or just plain observers and participants. However, Max Lerner warned us that the authentic élan (meaning "a feeling of commitment and of being on fire, a sense of mission, a sense that there are things worth living and dying for") of American civilization was "revolutionary" and told us that we should "stop being afraid of the term. . . ."[12] A passage from Yeats may be read as descriptive of the problems involved.

> *Turning and turning in the widening gyre*
> *The falcon cannot hear the falconer;*
> *Things fall apart; the center cannot hold;*
> *Mere anarchy is loosed upon the world,*
> *The blood-dimmed tide is loosed, and everywhere*
> *The ceremony of innocence is drowned;*
> *The best lack all conviction, while the worst*
> *Are full of passionate intensity.*[13]

The landmark study of equal educational opportunity in the United States was mandated by the Civil Rights Act of 1964 to the Commissioner of Education. The final report of this study became known as the Coleman report, after its principal investigator, Dr. James Coleman, of Johns Hopkins University. Coleman reports that "in planning the survey, it was obvious that no single concept of equality of educational opportunity existed. . . ."[14] Coleman then delineated those concepts he thought to be important.

[12]Max Lerner, "Humanist Goals," in Paul R. Hanna (ed.), *Education, An Instrument of National Goals,* McGraw-Hill, New York, 1962, pp. 105, 109. With permission.
[13]W. B. Yeats, "The Second Coming," in *The Collected Poems of W. B. Yeats,* Macmillan, New York, 1947, p. 215. With permission.
[14]Coleman, op. cit., p. 16.

The point of second importance in design [second to the point of discovering the intent of Congress, which was taken to be that the survey was not for the purpose of locating willful discrimination, but to determine educational inequality without regard to intention of those in authority] follows from the first and concerns the definition of inequality. One type of inequality may be defined in terms of differences of the community's input to the school, such as per pupil expenditure, school plants, libraries, quality of teachers, and other similar quantities.

A second type of inequality may be defined in terms of the racial composition of the school, following the Supreme Court's decision that segregated schooling is inherently unequal. By the former definition, the question of inequality through segregation is excluded, while by the latter, there is inequality of education within a school system so long as the schools within the system have different racial composition.

A third type of inequality would include various intangible characteristics of the school as well as the factors directly traceable to the community inputs to the school. These intangibles are such things as teacher morale, teachers' expectations of students, level of interest of the student body in learning, or others. Any of these factors may affect the impact of the school upon a given student within it. Yet such a definition gives no suggestion of where to stop, or just how relevant these factors might be for school quality.

Consequently, a fourth type of inequality may be defined in terms of consequences of the school for individuals with equal backgrounds and abilities. In this definition, equality of educational opportunity is equality of results, given the same individual input. With such a definition, inequality might come about from differences in the school inputs and/or racial composition and/or from more intangible things as described above.

Such a definition obviously would require that two steps be taken in the determination of inequality. First, it is necessary to determine the effect of these various factors upon educational results (conceiving of results quite broadly, including not only achievement but attitudes toward learning, self-image, and perhaps other variables). This provides various measures of the school's quality in terms of its effect upon its students. Second, it is necessary to take these measures of quality, once determined, and determine the differential exposure of Negroes (or other groups) and whites to schools of high and low quality.

A fifth type of inequality may be defined in terms of consequences of the school for individuals of unequal backgrounds and abilities. In this definition, equality of educational opportunity is equality of results given different individual inputs. The most striking examples of inequality here would be children from households in which a language other than English, such as Spanish or Navaho, is spoken. Other examples would be low-achieving children from homes in which there is a poverty of verbal expression or an absence of experiences which lead to conceptual facility.

Such a definition taken in the extreme would imply that educational equality is reached only when the results of schooling (achievement of attitudes) are the same for racial and religious minorities as for the dominant group.[15]

Coleman's definitions tend to minimize the impact of poverty. But it is clear that lifestyles imposed upon the poor are significant enough to cause differential school experiences between the poor and the nonpoor. It is also important to note that the poor today are not, for the most part, the traditional poor. Harrington calls them the "new" poor.

Indeed, one of the most important things about the new poverty is that it cannot be defined in simple statistical terms. . . . If a group has internal vitality, a will, if it has aspirations, it may suffer poverty, but it is not impoverished . . . but the new

[15]Coleman, op. cit., pp. 16–17. With permission.

> poverty is constituted to destroy aspiration; it is a system designed to be impervious to hope. The other America does not contain the adventurous seeking a new life and land. It is populated by the failures and by those driven from the land and bewildered by the city, by the old people suddenly confronted with the torments of loneliness and poverty, and by the minorities facing a wall of prejudice . . . these are the people who are immune to progress.[16]

The schools have done very little that recognizes such poverty. Let me be specific. First of all, education has always been sold as the open sesame to society, but schools have rarely produced the delivery systems to fulfill that promise. Schools are not even free. Many school districts, because of their peculiar financing patterns, charge students or their families for items or activities that are considered by both the school and the child as essential to the educational experience. In some places, this may be a charge for items as basic as books, or paper and pencils, or other instructional materials. Frequently, there is a requirement that all students will wear uniform special clothing in order to receive required physical education instruction, or there is a requirement that laboratory fees be paid before one can enroll in science courses. School dress codes may be such that only certain types of clothing are considered acceptable for attendance in school. Vital field trips and excursions may require a fee for admission or the bus ride, and fees for school photographs, class dues, entrance to athletic events, dances, even fees for bus transportation to and from school, may be required. In short, full participation in the educational program and important co-curriculum activities of the school most frequently requires the expenditure of some personal funds by the student or his family. In no state in this nation can a child fully participate in school without facing some or all of such expenditures. For the urban poor family

[16]Michael Harrington, *The Other America,* Penguin, Baltimore, 1964, pp. 17–19. With permission. Copyright © Michael Harrington, 1962, 1969.

with a number of children of school age, such expenses may constitute an extreme hardship, and for the child, the lack of appropriate funds, besides preventing his full participation, may be humiliating.

Child-welfare services, in many situations, have attempted to intervene. Welfare allowances are sometimes made for special clothing, school supplies, or school lunches. School health examinations may be provided free of charge at a public clinic, and sometimes, special welfare emergency funds are allocated to meet a particular crisis need, but many problems still arise. They are often the result of lack of information on the part of one agency as to what the other's procedures, requirements, and limitations are. The welfare agency has not anticipated the school's requirements, and the schools have not discovered the functional and financial limits of the welfare agency. In most cases, neither public institution is truly attentive and willing to take primary responsibility, perhaps because neither is supported adequately enough financially to respond to the total range of possible needs.

Perhaps one of the most significant characteristics of both institutionalized education and institutionalized child-welfare services is their depersonalized nature, evolved over the years. As is the case in many complex organizations, they have become self-defensive, self-perpetuating, and self-centered. Whenever an organization comes to view perpetuation of itself intact as a higher priority goal than the reason for which it was organized, its designated clientele inevitably suffers, since servicing its needs is no longer the primary motivation behind the organization's activity. Both schools and child-welfare agencies have been known to suffer from organizational paralysis, which inhibits their service to children and prevents or limits their collaboration with each other.

It is precisely the issues of *intent* and *intensity* of effort that may be the crux of the problem of dealing with the poor child or, indeed, any child now a victim of inequality. Coleman, after completing his study, concluded that "equality of output is not so much determined by equality of the resource inputs, but by the *power* of these resources in bringing about achievement."[17] The Dick and Jane school, in other words, is not committed to educating either the poor or the other nonmodel children. Neither does it relate empathetically to the communities from which such children come. Perhaps it does not even understand such communities, since the gulf between the middle-class, white school and any given poverty community is wide indeed. Henry S. Dyer, commenting on the Coleman data, suggests that:

> . . . the school characteristics that tend to be associated with differential levels of academic performance are not the sort that are readily affected by on-the-spot administrative decisions or by the spending of a little more money here and there. Many of them tend to be linked to the socioeconomic level of the pupil's parents and classmates; they tend to be the kind that are deeply rooted in the economic, social, and cultural level of the communities, and no important educational improvements in these schools are likely to take place until changes have occurred in the total community complex in which the schools are embedded.[18]

Surely it must be added that schoolpeople must know what is happening in their school's community, how it affects the children, and what the school can do to adjust to such realities. Dyer's conclusion should not relieve educators of responsibility to do something actively to change conditions. His conclusion must be construed as a challenge. A Watts resident once said to me:

> I can understand that people out in the San Fernando Valley don't care. They have never been here. They have never seen or

[17]Coleman, op. cit., p. 22.
[18]Henry S. Dyer, "School Factors and Equal Educational Opportunity," *Harvard Educational Review,* vol. 38, no. 1, p. 52, Winter 1968. With permission.

heard or smelled or touched shoulders with poverty. But I can't understand teachers and social workers and health people who come here everyday turning their backs on us. They know, and that knowledge should make for some concern, even obligation.

Education has always had the words for such commitment, even if it has not had the corresponding actions. Myron Lieberman was unkind enough to remind educators of their ethical obligations when he quoted the National Education Association's Code of Ethics. For example:

> **first principle**   The primary obligation of the teaching profession is to guide children, youth, and adults in the pursuit of knowledge and skills, to prepare them in the ways of democracy, and to help them become happy, useful, self-supporting citizens. The ultimate strength of the nation lies in the social responsibility, economic competence, and moral strength of the individual American. In fulfilling the obligations of this first principle, the teacher will . . .
>
> **1**   Deal justly and impartially with students regardless of their physical, mental, emotional, political, economic, social, racial, or religious characteristics.
>
> **2**   Recognize the differences among students and seek to meet their individual needs.[19]

It seems evident that educators have not lived up to such obligations. It is not clear whether the National Education Association ever vigorously supported this version of its own code. Certainly two factors have influenced the ability and will of education to respond. First, the code does not obligate administrators and other educational leaders in the same fashion that it does teachers. In hierarchial organizations, such an oversight is significant. Second,

[19]Myron Lieberman, *Education as a Profession,* Prentice-Hall, Englewood Cliffs, N.J., 1956, p. 422.

the economic and political pressures on teachers' organizations have directed much of their attention and energy toward the welfare problems of their members. Collective bargaining for teachers at all levels has become the major interest of professional education, and that activity tends to divert attention from the realities of the community and classroom as seen and lived by children and their parents.

Education, then, has become as privatistic as the general society. Nowhere is this clearer than in the responses to attempts to remove inequality of educational opportunity. It should be self-evident that the enormity of offense committed upon the poor and the minorities in this country over the past 200 years should be moral argument enough to insist that such offense cease and desist at once and that all possible restitution be granted immediately. To do less makes us warlords of a realm that defies all the precepts of our Constitution as well as the basic tenets of Christian-Hebraic culture. Nevertheless, when desegregation was declared the law of the land, the resistance to change was sharp and angry. Attention in the 1950s and 1960s was focused on the seventeen southern and border states where segregation had been *de jure* (by law) rather than *de facto* (in fact). There was much violence and people were actually killed during the period of adjustment.

The Supreme Court ruled that there was not equal educational opportunity in segregated schools and that this form of social inequality must stop. Although the resistance continued, the schools had to be integrated. Conflict over the Court's decision is now centered on the issue of *busing,* although the transportation by bus of children in sparsely settled areas has gone on for more than half a century. Everyone seems to have forgotten that in segregation days children, both black and white, walked or were bused past the closest school to attend one that was segregated. In southwest Birmingham, Alabama, for example, black students who now walk to their integrated high schools (their neighborhood high schools, in fact) had to give up traveling by bus to their former all-black schools.

In Willie Morris's eloquent story of the integration of the schools in Yazoo City, Mississippi,[20] there is no mention of busing, or walking, or any other method of integration, only the agonies of the achievement of the social purpose of desegregation. For some, integration has come to mean riding a bus in a different direction to a new destination or, perhaps, riding a bus for the first time, even though the busing of children to school has a long history in American education and is a major form of transportation all over the nation.

In fact, busing was used years ago to extend educational opportunity to children in rural areas too sparsely populated to maintain the urban-suburban institution of the neighborhood school. There is no evidence that any of these rural children were intellectually or emotionally damaged by this busing experience. Indeed, the experience was so successful that urban and suburban school districts began to use buses themselves, where attendance areas of "neighborhood" schools were too large to require that all children walk to school. It is common today to find both rural and urban school districts with fleets of buses. They may transport children to and from school when distances warrant it, and they may be used to take children from school to out-of-school educational experiences such as concerts, museums, and other extending activities. Private and parochial school systems also use extensive busing to service their schools, since, in most places, such systems do not have enough schools to have "neighborhood" schools. There is no record of protest over these traditional uses of buses, except perhaps when someone gets left out.

Busing became controversial only when it became a primary method of achieving integration. If the social purpose of assuring equal educational opportunity through integration could have been achieved by equal economic opportunity and open housing for minority groups, then the busing issue would have become irrelevant. In other words, busing is only a temporary

[20]Willie Morris, *Yazoo,* Harper & Row, New York, 1971.

measure to be used until the other disparities are removed. Perhaps walking will become the primary method of achieving integration. It is to be hoped that there would be no national campaign by irate and politically sensitive congressmen against walking and no mysterious midnight dynamiting of children's shoes.

Busing was always acceptable, even worthy of a Norman Rockwell kind of enshrinement as a part of Americana, until it became a symbol of racial integration. Antagonism toward busing came from blacks who felt that busing should involve both races and from whites who objected to its use to achieve integration. The most virulent opposition to busing has been, of course, racist, but one must concede that another set of feelings may sometimes be involved. The sense of neighborhood, deeply embedded in the growth of American cities, is thought by some to be violated by busing. This means a threat to their identity and to whatever values living in a certain neighborhood may support. For example, some people feel that they have worked hard, even sacrificed, to achieve a place in a certain neighborhood and that others who have not gone through the same struggle should not be permitted to use that neighborhood's facilities (in this case, the school). Others view their neighborhood as an identity, perhaps because it is the only identity they have or because the area has some homogeneity of race or ethnic origin. In 1971, the Chinese in San Francisco vehemently resisted the busing of their children out of the Chinese neighborhood as well as the busing of non-Chinese into "their" schools. "Cultural identity" was given as the excuse for this resistance.

It is interesting to note that there is no research to indicate that the neighborhood school is necessarily better or worse than any other organizational scheme, if we talk in educational terms. Part of the reason for this is, of course, the difficulty in defining a school neighborhood: Attendance areas change with the need to achieve numerical balance; and the neighborhood changes definition when a child moves from elementary school to junior high school to high school. For these reasons, the campaign against busing cannot legitimately be based upon protecting the sanctity of what is, at best, a hypothetical neighborhood school. Proposals in Congress to actually outlaw busing by constitutional amendment confirm that it is not busing that offends, but what busing can achieve. A common wording of such proposed amendments reads: "No public school student shall, because of his race, creed, or color, be assigned or required to attend a particular school."

Note that neither busing nor walking nor any other method is mentioned. An amendment so worded could, and probably would in some places, permit instant resegregation, given maintenance of present segregated housing patterns. Court orders could omit reference to busing, but in order to achieve desegregation (clearly the law), some method would have to be used. It is the issue of equal educational opportunity achieved through integration that remains the real cause for the controversy over busing. Busing, per se, is simply being used as a thin excuse to divert this country from achieving a major and long overdue social change. The resistance to integration, of course, was enhanced by the refusal of school authorities to consider seriously any other method but busing. Cities that had other means of transportation (subways or other systems of rapid transit) spoke only of busing. School planners did not consider relocating new schools to make them more accessible to both biracial housing or established transportation routes. City planners tended to ignore relocation of schools too, since relationships between school planners and city planners in most cities have never been intimate. One urban superintendent came up with the slogan "Quality education for all children where they are." As is the case with slogans, definition is vague. This slogan turned out in practice to mean that the schools will try to do the "best" (undefined) they can for all children, provided that doing the "best" does not disturb the status quo, socially, politically, or economically. The practical results in this particular district are clear: Of the larger urban school systems in America, it is now one of the five most segregated.

Another major obstacle to integration, by busing or otherwise, has been the growing advocacy of community control, which means control at the neighborhood level. I will discuss this later.

In general, poverty is the closest thing to a common denominator for groups that are adversely affected by inequality of educational opportunity. The issue of social class or *classism* is fundamental and often overrides its more commonly recognized correlative, racism. Social stratification in the United States is largely on a socioeconomic scale; the richer you are, the higher on the scale, and conversely, the poorer you are, the less prestige and power you have. Thus the middle-class school looks askance at poor whites as well as poor blacks, or browns, or any other racial minorities. Middle-class blacks look down on lower-class blacks even as they are themselves victimized by racism, despite their socioeconomic class. The difference between classism and racism is, of course, that classism can be overcome, at least in theory; racism cannot, at least not by the victims. The solutions are different, but are often viewed as similar. Classism is economic and therefore is subject to economic solutions. Racism, on the other hand, is psychological and political and rarely yields to economic solutions, just as classism rarely succumbs to purely political or social solutions.

Inequality has many faces and many moods. It can rise and fall with time and circumstance; it can shift with the winds of economic stress or social derangement. If schools should continue to be organized to maximize student alienation, inequality of educational opportunity could infect almost any group or class. But the groups most commonly and persistently aggrieved are the blacks, the Spanish-speaking, the Native Americans, the poor whites, and the immigrant ethnics. Each group has some distinct differences from the others, and each maintains its own set of obsessions and aspirations. Rarely have the five groups worked cooperatively to remove the causes of their common disadvantages.

Blacks, or Negroes, or Afro-Americans, identified here by whatever term is acceptable to them, are considered to be the largest minority group in the United States and are the most consistently victimized by racism and inequality. In the past twenty-five years, blacks have entered a transitional period and, as an organized subculture, tend to be in a state of disarray. This is not entirely unexpected, nor is it necessarily a deficit. Even though the increments of progress are often painfully small and seemingly amorphous, there have been considerable changes in the general status of blacks since World War II. The war effort itself, because of the need for total citizen involvement, broke down some of the patterns of racial isolation. The postwar civil-rights movement, most generously influenced by the leadership of Martin Luther King and the legal activities of the NAACP, sped the cause further. In the great surge for equality, many blacks were subjected to rapid and profound changes, and, as human beings, and as other groups have done, they reacted with varying degrees of accommodation to those changes. Many older blacks, for example, could not adjust quickly and still display some reservations about what has and is happening. On the other hand, many young blacks reacted with explosive force, running the range of responses from angry, hostile militancy to bewilderment to industrious opportunism in the dominant white system.

Since there are so many different kinds of blacks[21] and so many different responses, both in degree and kind, the transitional period was almost bound to display some confusion. The black movement, as it symbolizes the equalitarian thrust of recent years, inevitably contained all of the ambiguities of any such social movement. To be politically effective, it must have more sharply defined goals than just the claim to equality. To be socially and

[21]See Charles Valentine, "Deficit, Difference, and Bicultural Models of Afro-American Behavior," *Harvard Educational Review,* vol. 41, May 1971, and the rejoinder to Valentine by Simpkins, Williams, and Gunnings in the November 1971 issue (vol. 41).

economically effective, it must face the reality that to succeed it must dislodge some incumbent socioeconomic power. To succeed educationally, it must devise a new system that is effective for its children and have sufficient control over schools to assure its implementation. Even more importantly, and perhaps most difficult, it must learn to distinguish between friends and enemies. Not all differences with the black movement are illegitimate and racist.

There are many crucial decisions yet to be made. Do blacks want to become a part of the present system? If so, are there not some fundamental contradictions that must be rationalized? If one accepts the notion that the present system of schooling is largely a social control device that has traditionally excluded blacks, how can blacks now accept such a system and want to be a part of it? More specifically, if the present educational system is premised upon the learners' being essentially white-enculturated, middle-class-socialized, and professional lifestyle-oriented, how will blacks invade such a system without compromising their own identity and perhaps destroying it? If, on the other hand, blacks desire to enter a revised system, what should the revisions be? Will it be integration, separation, or some combination of the two? Who should be the architects? At present, these discussions have not been made in any fashion that suggests a unity of purpose and desire. Perhaps such unity is not desirable, since individual blacks may want to remain individuals first and blacks second.

When black leaders announced the political slogan "We have no permanent friends or permanent enemies, only permanent interests," they perhaps should have remembered another slogan, long associated with Samuel Gompers and the labor movement: "Reward your friends and punish your enemies." It should be pointed out that the labor movement is the only lower-class-originated social movement ever to succeed in the United States, and the Gompers slogan was important to that success because it promoted social, economic, and political alliances of trust and mutual interest. The black slogan, on the other hand, offers no assurances or recognition of mutuality. It is a brave position, but it may be inherently ineffective because, as has already occurred, blacks who do not reciprocate loyalties and remain unnecessarily independent cannot reasonably expect to retain the friends they had during the peak years of the civil-rights movement.

It seems to me that the black leaders should have also considered the idea that their rugged independence also tends to mean isolation and separation which, in turn, means entering a highly competitive political and socioeconomic system at the peak of disadvantage. The moral issues that Dr. King raised and so relentlessly used to press for progress are squandered away. This black thrust for power and equality becomes just another entry in a competitive system that has, historically, stacked the race against blacks. In other words, why make the task more difficult? Or, as Robert Frost said:

> *Before I built a wall I'd ask to know*
> *What I was walling in or walling out,*
> *And to whom I was like to give offense.*

What then constitutes educational coexistence? This question takes on additional nuances when we consider still other oppressed groups.

The Spanish-speaking, a heterogeneous group made up of at least the Chicanos of the Southwest, the Puerto Ricans of the East and Midwest, the Cubans of Florida, and the Filipinos of central California, represent another facet of the problem of inequality. It is clear that because of race, enculturation into a distinctive subculture, and language, the Spanish-speaking have been systematically rejected by the Dick and Jane school. Their isolation has often been both physical and intellectual. Actually, one of the first desegregation decisions of the federal courts came in 1945 when Judge Paul J.

McCormick of the U.S. District Court ruled that separate facilities for Mexican-American children in Orange County, California, deprived those children "of a common cultural attitude" and ruled an end to such practices. The McCormick decision in the Mendez case was upheld by the Ninth Circuit Court on April 14, 1947. (D.C.Cal., 64 F. Supp. 55, 161 F. 2d 774.) Yet it was in 1965, twenty years later, that Congress passed Title VII of the Elementary and Secondary Education Act of 1965 (the Bilingual Education Act), thus officially and nationally recognizing the problem of bilingualism.

The inequality of educational opportunity for the Spanish-speaking was only partly redressed by the recognition of bilingualism as a problem. There has been little reorganization of schools or their curricular premises to deal with biculturalism and to confront the inherent racism that marked the exclusion of many Spanish-speaking. Again, the system was not organized to *maintain* cultural variances; on the contrary, it was organized to expunge such differences. The national doctrines of assimilation and amalgamation could not have had it any other way. That American schools could have so effectively suppressed this large minority group's legitimate interests for so long, considering the close proximity of the Latin American world and the authentic heritage of the Southwest, is testimonial to the power of the "Anglo" vision of propriety.

I was in a California school district in the mid 1960s where 84 percent of the enrollment was natively Spanish-speaking, and yet there were no bicultural or bilingual materials used; in fact, they were specifically forbidden. Teaching English as a second language was unknown, and all reporting systems to parents were carried out in English on the grounds that the district "could not cater to its Latin population." The results of such discrimination against the Spanish-speaking have been dramatic. In one Midwestern city, the dropout rate among Puerto Ricans has never been less than 90 percent. The 1960 census indicated that some 20 percent fewer Chicano youths, aged sixteen and seventeen, were in school than were their Anglo counterparts. The story is endless; it is being documented daily by scholars and writers who, in the past ten years, have become concerned about "the Forgotten Americans."[22]

The problem of the Spanish-speaking people confronting both the general community and the school has become, as with blacks, a question of goals. "Brown power," or "taco power," needs direction and consideration of the same underlying questions that face all minority groups. Do they want into a system that is premised upon their being out? Confronting the educational system with nationalistic slogans and unfocused militancy will probably result in little progress. Rather, clear statements of clear educational goals are needed, and these must be related to the realities of the bicultural, bilingual community. Such goals and the educational techniques of implementation are not unknown. Much work is being done at the Southwestern Cooperative Educational Laboratory in Albuquerque, New Mexico, and at Western Regional School Desegregation Projects at the University of California at Riverside.[23] An extensive study was done in New York City on teaching Puerto Ricans,[24] but it has not had the impact that was anticipated by its

[22]The reader should consult such volumes as: Julian Samora (ed.), *La Raza: Forgotten Americans,* University of Notre Dame Press, South Bend, Ind., 1966; Celia S. Heller, *Mexican-American Youth,* Random House, New York, 1966; John H. Burma (ed.), *Mexican-Americans in the United States,* Schenkman, Cambridge, Mass., 1970; Stan Steiner, *La Raza,* Harper & Row, New York, 1970; Oscar Lewis, *La Vida,* Random House, New York, 1965; Patricia Sexton, *Spanish Harlem: Anatomy of Poverty,* Harper & Row, New York, 1965; and Clarence Senior, *The Puerto Ricans,* Quadrangle, Chicago, 1965.
[23]See Atilano A. Valencia, *Bilingual/Bicultural Education: A Quest for Institutional Reform,* Intergroup Bulletin Series, Riverside, Calif., April 1971; also Roger M. Baty, *Education for Cultural Awareness,* Intergroup Bulletin Series, Riverside, Calif., June 1971.
[24]See J. Cayce Morrison, *The Puerto Rican Study,* Board of Education, New York, 1958.

authors. Solutions to the technical problems of teaching English as a second language are also well known[25] even if they are not always implemented. In short, these are problems in which the will is more in question than the way.

The problem of equal educational opportunity for the Native American or Indian is much more complex. At the outset, the term "Indian" is a misnomer foisted upon the natives of the Western Hemisphere by European explorers whose knowledge of world geography was limited. Such inability to distinguish between cultures has persisted so that even today the some six hundred different native groups with at least two hundred different languages are still called by the single term, Indian. No group has less known about it or more misconceptions perpetrated on it. In short, all most Americans know is that, as the old saying goes, "all Indians walk in single file, or at least the one I saw did."

A few brief but sorry statistics tell the story of the poorest of the poor in the United States.

> Their average life expectancy is 63.9 years; for *all* other Americans, it is 70.
>
> Their average annual income, $1,500, is 75% less than the national average, and $1,000 below that of the average black family.
>
> Their unemployment rate is nearly 40%, about ten times the national average.
>
> Fifty thousand Indian families live in grossly substandard houses, many without running water, electricity, or adequate sanitary facilities.

[25]See Mary Finocchiaro, *Teaching English as a Second Language*, rev. and enl., new, Harper & Row, New York, 1969. Also, Thomas D. Horn (ed.), *Reading for the Disadvantaged: Problems of the Linguistically Different Learners*, Harcourt Brace Jovanovich, Inc., New York, 1970.

Their infant mortality after the first month of life is three times the national average.

Fifty percent of Indian schoolchildren, double the national average, drop out, or more properly stated, are pushed out by inadequate educational systems before they complete high school.

The suicide rate of Indian teen-agers is one hundred times that of whites . . .[26]

If any group of Americans has been subjected to deliberate governmental policies of near genocide, it has been the Native American. At first, the policy was to isolate by force by crowding Native Americans onto reservations, areas of land that seemed to be of no use to whites. Then, in the spirit of assimilation, there was the Dawes General Allotment Act of 1887, which tried to break up reservations, thus making each Native American family a small landowner, but leaving such families unprotected from an economic system that almost guaranteed that they would be unable to maintain such allotments. It was not until 1934 and the passage of the Wheeler Howard Act (Indian Reorganization Act) that the damaging process was stopped, or at least slowed down.

As for education, excerpts of the report of the Special Subcommittee on Education in 1969, chaired by the late Senator Robert Kennedy, tell a sad tale.

. . . The school buildings themselves; the course materials and books; the attitudes of teachers and administrative personnel; the accessibility of school buildings . . . all these are of shocking quality.

[26]Alvin M. Josephy, Jr., *Red Power: The American Indians' Fight for Freedom,* American Heritage, New York, 1971, p. 15.

The average educational level for all Indians under Federal supervision is 5 school years;

More than one out of five of every five Indian men have less than 5 years of schooling;

The average age of top level Bureau of Indian Affairs education administrators is 58 years;

Only 18% of the students in Federal Indian schools go on to college . . . only 3% graduate.

The BIA spends only $18 per year per child on textbooks and supplies.

Only one of the 226 BIA schools is governed by an elective school board.[27]

Obviously the first task of those asking for equal educational opportunity for Native Americans is a drastic reorganization of their schooling patterns and a massive infusion of financial resources to that process. The Senate subcommittee also recommended that this should not be done without extensive participation in the deliberations by Native Americans themselves. Ultimately any decisions reached should be subject to the ratification of those most directly affected.

The second task to confront would be the incredibly complex linguistic problem. It seems clear that no single educational prescription (as we in American education are wont to propose) will come close to attending to the teaching-learning problems of such diverse groups. Needless to say, there are hundreds of persons needed to devise perhaps two hundred different systems of education that would account for both the linguistic and cultural differences among Native Americans without, at any time or in any way,

[27] *1969 Report of the U.S. Senate Committee on Labor and Public Welfare,* made by its Special Subcommittee on Indian Education, Washington, D.C., 1969.

devaluing or expunging any group's identity, right of self-determination (freedom), or cultural aspirations (including religion). Native American young people are obviously the greatest single potential source of such personnel, but the challenge to educational sociologists, or educational anthropologists, or linguists is also there. The intent of such activity, of course, would have to be action, not mere study. Native Americans have been studied ad nauseum; a Navaho girl once remarked to me that it seemed as though the average Navaho family consisted of a father, a mother, two children, and an anthropologist.

The Senate subcommittee stated: "In conclusion, it is sufficient to restate our basic finding; that our Nation's policies and programs for educating American Indians are a national tragedy. They present us with a national challenge of no small proportions . . ."[28]

In the cases of the three groups just described, racism was a significant factor affecting their inequality. For the poor-white group, the issue is clearly classism. Harrington identifies many of the poor white as recognizable by their "9th generation Anglo-Saxon faces, the accents, and . . . their country music."[29] This description would be limited, of course, to Appalachians, the Arkansas-Oklahoma-Texas sharecroppers and cotton pickers, migrants (usually Southern and Southwestern), and the generally rural white poor. But the poor white is also urban (displaced by technology), and he or she may be aged (visit any number of small downtown hotels). The poor in the United States are about three times more likely to be white than nonwhite. Of the more than $2^{1}/_{2}$ million people on welfare, a clear majority are white.

In a sense, one might define the contemporary poor in the United States as those who, for reasons beyond their control, cannot help themselves. All the most decisive factors making

[28]Ibid.
[29]Michael Harrington, *The Other America*, Penguin, Baltimore, 1964, p. 96.

for opportunity and advance are against them. They are born going downward, and most of them stay down. They are victims whose lives are endlessly blown round and round the other America.[30]

The poor white tends to be invisible to the average middle-class American. For one reason, he is usually not dressed in rags like a character out of Dickens. For another, he tends to live apart; he is more often rural or at least nonurban, but even if he lives in the city, it is rarely in the teeming minority ghettos so often thought of as symbolic of the urban poor. And too, the poor white is often mobile, a nomad following crops or rumors of a job or dreams of a new start. If he is average, the head of the poor family in 61 percent of the cases has had eight years or less of education, and he and his family may earn less than $3000 per year. If he is a migrant, he may earn only 50¢ an hour, or about $600 per year per worker as of 1959. That may be closer to $1000 a year in 1971.

The poor white is not the classic poor person of old. He is a displaced person, a reject, a person lost in the thickets of an increasingly impersonal, profit-oriented, technological society. The technological revolution surely accounts for much of the displacement: Mechanized, corporate farming, a change in fuels, and increased automation of the manufacturing processes. The small family farmer who could not compete, the farm worker, the coal miner, and the textile worker, all have lost their utility and have been cast off.

Education is, of course, one of those "most decisive factors for opportunity" that Harrington claims have been working against the poor white.[31] Certainly, the middle-class neighborhood school with its assumption of population stability has done little for such people. It is not known at this time whether the poor whites,

[30]Ibid., p. 15.
[31]Ibid.

particularly those in rural areas or the mountains, have any faith left in either the educational process or its outcomes. Eating has usually had a higher priority than schooling; and chronic despair can impair even the most determined optimist.

The final group for discussion are the ethnics, who are not necessarily victims of racism, but in their own perception, they are being jostled a bit too much by classism.

> We pay good money for education, but do not receive good education in return. The schools fail to prepare our children for college. They lack vocational programs. They have no outreach programs in our communities. If our children are accepted for college, the tuition makes it impossible for many of them to attend.[32]

These are working-class people who still maintain their ethnic identity, usually European. They do not wish to lose that identity, and are increasingly militant about building a culturally pluralistic society. Certainly language and culture have tended to hamper their progress in the Anglo-Saxon–oriented school, so much so that they are asking for more comparative ethnic-cultural studies programs in schools.

There are additional groups that are now asserting their existence as distinctive subcultures largely overlooked or misinterpreted by the school system. One of the most significant of these is the Asian-American, which, in fact, is composed of still other subgroupings such as the Chinese-Americans and the Japanese-Americans.[33]

The emergence of "ethnic power" is stark proof of the

[32]From *Ethnos,* the Bulletin of the National Center for Urban Ethnic Affairs, Washington, D.C., July 1971. With permission.
[33]See Ben R. Tong, "The Ghetto of the Mind," *Amerasia Journal,* vol. 3, November 1971.

failure of both the assimilation and amalgamation models and reminds us once again of the reality of cultural pluralism in America.

> You know, Mrs. Shakespeare, the world has become so small that different standards and different concepts are forced into good neighborliness when they have absolutely nothing in common. There are so many anomalies these days that the quantity of conceivable disasters has increased to a frightening extent. I am haunted by any amount of eventualities, and open my paper every morning with a gathering sense of foreboding.[34]

Sir Neville's outlook may be a bit bleak, but surely it has been demonstrated that America is blessed (or cursed) with incredible diversity. Cultural pluralism then is a fact, not an amendable social policy. As an individual, one may deal with a fact or ignore it; there are perils either way. Education, however, as an organized activity, cannot avoid reality; such dissociation contains the seeds of its own destruction. The school's franchise, no matter what your view, has always argued that it should prepare children and youth to work and live in the society. If that society is pluralistic (and we have established that ours is), then the only way a school can prepare a student to cope with that society is to recognize pluralism and teach accordingly. Any other procedure, including coerced assimilation or amalgamation, would be folly.

> What is important, however, is the fact that uniformity is superimposed, not inwardly generated. Under its regimentation the diversities persist; upon it and by means of it they grow. But instead of growing freely, and fusing by their own expansion into contact and harmony with their peers, they grow distortedly, as reactions against and compensations for the superimposed unity. In the end they must win free, for Nature is naturally pluralistic; her unities are eventual, not primary; natural adjust-

[34]So says Sir Neville in Peter Ustinov's novel, *Krumnagel,* Atlantic Monthly, Boston, 1971, p. 95. With permission.

ments not regimentation of superior force. Human institutions have the same character. *Where there is no mutuality, there may be "law and order" but there cannot be peace.*[35] [Italics added.]

Mutuality must, of course, be defined as dynamic, because any adventure involving many races, many cultures, many lifestyles, all coexisting within the framework of American democracy, cannot be static; indeed, the strength of such a society rests upon dynamism.

Pluralism also implies a parity of power, mutually respected, lest the nation continue to shatter itself with endless competitive polarizations. There is an underlying futility in attempting, as we have in the past, to build some sort of single, monolithic culture. It is impossible to suppress the diverse individual strands that made the American experiment in heterogeneity unique. Neither is it possible to permanently subordinate any one group to another. Indeed, the eruptions of suppressed groups in our recent history prove that the suppressors were wrong, not the suppressed.

Education, as an instrument of national goals, is therefore committed to creating effective educational environments that support racial and cultural pluralism. The alternative would be to prepare children and youth for a world that does not exist; some young people are saying that that is precisely what American education has been doing, and that is why they are revolting. The task of preparing youth for cultural pluralism, therefore, is inescapable.[36]

[35]Horace Kallen, *Culture and Democracy in the United States,* Boni and Liveright, New York, 1924, pp. 178–179. With permission. Copyright © by Horace Kallen.

[36]The reader who is still unconvinced is invited to read Seymour Itzkoff, *Cultural Pluralism and American Education,* International Textbook, Scranton, Pa., 1969; Saul D. Feldman and Gerald W. Thielbar, *Life Styles: Diversity in American Society,* Little, Brown, Boston, 1972; David Nalloway and Francesco Cordasco, *Minorities and the American City,* McKay, New York, 1970; and special issue, "Imperatives in Ethnic Minority Education," *Phi Delta Kappan,* vol. 53, no. 5, January 1972.

A plan to provide effective education for cultural pluralism[37] would need to permeate the entire operation of a school district. This is to say that education for cultural pluralism would be a controlling purpose of the district and would be diffused into all aspects of each school and its programs, including staffing, student-staff relationships, the curriculum, the extracurricular activities, personal interactions, teaching methodology, and community relations.

Obviously such education should bring together students and staff or differing races and cultures for both planned and spontaneous activities that celebrate the autonomy of each group. The school would seek to overcome any limitations on student and staff diversity that are the result of geography or residential patterns. Within most urban communities, this should not be too difficult, if there is the will to extend real opportunities for significant multicultural and multiracial education. Any present racism or classism, either overt or covert, should be confronted honestly, just as the racism and classism implicit in many of our present institutional forms would be acknowledged and corrected.

Specifically, such a program would embrace at least the following educational commitments:

1 *Multicultural and multiracial education should recognize a significant diversity of students; therefore, programs for students should be highly individualized.*

Some educators may prefer the phrase *personalized learning* to the usual *individualized instruction* on the grounds that ultimately it is the learning of the student that is more important than the instruction of the teacher. One would suspect that effective

[37]Much of the thinking in this plan emerged from the working sessions of the Task Force on Multi-Cultural/Multi-Racial Education of the National Study of School Evaluation. My colleagues on that task force were John Stanavage, Chairman, Richard Foster, Charles Baltimore, Father John Fahey, and David Gifford.

individualized instruction eventually becomes personalized learning, but it is worthwhile to indicate that there may be a difference, since instruction implies some kind of expertise or authority, and the imposition of the schools' authority has often been the source of many of our difficulties. The task of implementing individualization has been made easier by the growing experience of educators with nongraded elementary schools, individualized reading programs, modular scheduling, and many computer-derived innovations. The central point is that the school would, at last, recognize and honor differences.

2   *Estimates of ability should be based on results and instruments that have no socioeconomic, race, or cultural bias. Such estimates should be applied to the widest possible variety of achievements.*

The challenge here involves the whole conceptualization of testing and standards. We have long known that our estimates of a student's ability and achievement have been pretty much limited to that which we could test, or thought we could test. The limitations of such an approach were further increased by the implicit desire for a standardized procedure that could be applied to all. Standardized tests of a narrow spectrum of learning activity almost inevitably introduced significant socioeconomic, racial, and cultural biases, even as they implicitly violated the individual learner's autonomy. However, it must be said that we can devise meaningful evaluations of students without resorting to the discredited assumption of a need for standardized or uniform results. It will be difficult for some educators to break their habits, and special care will be needed for them during the withdrawal period.

3   *The school recognizes and values different learning styles, different vocational goals, and different life purposes. The school will not insist upon any universal "best" model.*

As was said earlier, standardization implies some single model, some ideal prototype against which all are to be judged. It should be clear that no such model exists in a culturally pluralistic society. The recognition and celebration of diversity specifically legislates against any universal optimum student or teacher. We are gradually learning that there can be joy and fulfillment in many lifestyles and roles. It is only when we insist upon stratifying such styles and roles that we breed discontent, inequality, and alienation. Who is to say that the way of the Hopi (meaning *peaceful*) is any greater or lesser than the way of the Bohanna (meaning *white man*)?

4   *The processes by which students learn social behavior both emphasize and value diverse cultural definitions of social behavior.*

   The restrained decorum characteristic of the true Dick and Jane school is not necessarily appropriate in all multicultural settings. It may be too restrictive even for Dick and Jane. The school's role in teaching social behaviors should not exceed its right to impose minimum behavioral standards. This is to say that the school cannot presume to insist that all people must react to social intercourse in any singular mode beyond that which is necessary for all to survive. If there are behavioral differences that emerge naturally from legitimate cultural differences, they need to be celebrated rather than suppressed. Students who face a lifetime in a pluralistic society need to learn how to cope with associates who display alternative modes of response to social interaction, in language, manners, even moral codes of conduct. In this context, *machismo,* for example, may be considered an asset rather than a liability.

5   *While insisting upon behavior that is neither antisocial nor hostile to any other group, the school is tolerant of behavior differences.*

   This extends the concepts embedded in point 4 and suggests that limitations may be imposed, but never thoughtlessly or merely to suit the personal taste and convenience of school authorities. The word *tolerant* is not to imply the treatment or differences as quaint or odd, as frequently happens when a teacher shows her own obvious distaste, but nobly and with great sacrifice manages to permit such behavior to persist. Rather the school *deliberately* seeks out cultural variation and attempts to assure in each student a mutual acceptance of differences.

6   *At no time and in no way should the school attempt to devalue or expunge the cultural heritage of any student, staff member, or member of the community.*

This injunction is the essence of multicultural education. Its purpose is to finally lay to rest all past and futile attempts at assimilation or amalgamation. The positive analogue would be the growth of both minority and majority studies designed to promote an unbiased view of history, both in the affective and cognitive senses of self and others, and the obliteration of ethnic oppression in any form. Some less than definitive examples might be: (1) Remembering to honor the Native American child's heritage by not insisting that Columbus discovered America; (2) seriously investigating the *West* African civilizations from which most American blacks came. (And, incidentally, not confusing this issue by superimposing *East* African languages and customs as a substitute heritage); (3) looking for contributions like the German import of the mid nineteenth century, the kindergarten, or the Mexican hacienda organization that became the organizational pattern for most Western ranches, or any number of the authentic and dignified assets of our diverse population groups. In a sense, multicultural education seeks to rediscover the soul of America at the same time that it assures every child of a positive self-image and a sense of his own unique antecedents.

7   *Teaching methodologies that instruct a student in his own culture (enculturation) may differ from those that instruct him in another culture (acculturation). The school staff should be sensitive to when and where the use of each of these kinds of methods is appropriate.*

The most obvious example of this concept is found in the teaching of language. At present, and despite the limited application of the Bilingual Education Act, most schools with, say, predominately Spanish-speaking enrollments, teach in English and do so on the assumption that the learner is a native English-speaker. Indeed, most textbooks used in American schools make a similar assumption with the obvious consequence that they do not deal with the problems of English faced by a non native English-speaker.

> There are inherent differences between English and other languages that are likely to cause distortions of juncture, syntax, and emphasis. Attempts by the non-English-speaking child at word attack may be severely inhibited by his difficulties in enunciation and his lack of general English language experience.[38]

An Anglo teacher once complained about Eduardo's progress: "He doesn't know his sounds." The multicultural educator would reply that Eduardo, in fact, does know *his* sounds, but he may not know the teacher's.

Some schools go halfway. They offer English as a Second Language (ESL) to non-English-speakers during a part of the school day, but the rest of the day, they treat such a learner as if he were a native speaker. ESL is acculturational, while the regularly scheduled program is enculturational. Schools must know the difference and teach accordingly lest they imply some inherent disadvantage and dishonor in being a nonmodel (not an Anglo-English-speaking) child.

8   *Teaching methodologies place high priority upon building a sense of personal worth in each student, both as an individual and as a member of a distinct cultural/racial group.*

Certainly the equal distribution of power and prestige to all groups will build a sense of security and worthiness in each member of each group, insofar as their group identity is the question. Given true equal educational opportunity, a child's ethnicity or social

[38]Louis Fischer and Donald R. Thomas, *Social Foundations of Educational Decisions,* Wadsworth, Belmont, Calif., 1965, p. 219. With permission.

class should no longer be a deterrent to his achievement. At the outset, the redistribution of power and prestige will need sensitive understanding. Some groups will have to yield power; others will taste it for the first time and may not use it with experience and wisdom. Conflicts may arise, but schools may view such tensions as creative opportunities in multicultural education. Conflict management, so often the technique used by schools, is inappropriate and ultimately hurtful. As has been said, "where there is no mutuality, there may be 'law and order' but there cannot be peace."[39]

The objectives of multicultural and multiracial education (and I am thinking of multisocial class as derivative of multicultural) are to have students emerge from the educational process with demonstrable understanding of our democratic pluralistic society. Behaviorally, that might mean:

1   They establish friendships, both in and out of school, that freely cross cultural, racial, and social-class lines.

2   They elect and support fellow students in leadership roles with a fairly equal distribution of the various cultural and racial groups in the school.

3   They seek cross-cultural experiences in the school curriculum.

4   They express approval of any achievement, individual or group, without ethnic or class bias.

The school that emerges as a truly pluralistic organization displays some definite characteristics.

1   It provides an organization that recognizes all cultural and racial differences and distributes its resources, power, and prestige among such groups.

[39]Kallen, op. cit., p. 179.

2   It provides an instructional program that serves the needs and aspirations of each cultural and racial group without violating the integrity of any other group.

3   It provides a climate and a program in which all students can learn about cultural and racial differences and are given practical opportunities to demonstrate, celebrate, and maintain those differences.

4   It engages in frequent communication with the community, both on the individual and group level, concerning all aspects of school and community life as they relate to multicultural education.

5   It readily accepts mutual participation of school and community as contributing decision makers in the various multicultural experiences each is providing children and youth.

6   It shares with the community a mutual concern for the correction of those conditions within the community or within the school that deny equal opportunity to any student.

7   It expresses approval and support for the contributions made by the community to multicultural education.

8   It provides an organizational structure for cooperative decision-making among all cultural and racial groups in the community with regard to the school's program, activities, and procedures.

9   It provides an organizational structure that responds adequately to changing conditions and needs in the community.

To accomplish these goals, the school must totally reassess its operation, even the knowledge it has of its community and its students. Comprehensive demographic data, continually updated, is an essential component. If such study shows a narrow range of class, cultural, and racial differences, such *homogeneity should be viewed with alarm,* since it would tend to defeat the achievement of a truly pluralistic learning environment.

The philosophy of multicultural education, as I have said, would need to permeate the entire school or school district. This means that schools would examine the way multicultural goals are reflected in board actions, the central administration, the individual school staff, as well as among the students. Personnel policies would be affected at all staff levels, certified or noncertified. Obviously, much emphasis would be placed on the quality, the attitudes, the skills, and the commitments of the teachers, guidance personnel, and any other staff members intimately involved with students. The school's curriculum would also be examined to assure that it reflected multicultural goals in every area of study. Learning materials and library holdings would be carefully assessed for the maximum range of multicultural and multiracial emphasis. Extracurricular activities would provide unique opportunities to further multicultural goals, as would all activities where student involvement was implicit.

The attainment of equal educational opportunity depends upon recognition of diversity first, in all its aspects, and then deliberate action to sustain that diversity with honor. The importance of being equal is that it may be the only way America and each of us can survive.

chapter four

schools:
a challenge to
organizational
theory

Schools are formal organizations. The fact that they are not currently functioning appropriately sets forth a challenge to amend or modify that formal organization. Organizational change involving people and their social arrangements is never simple, particularly if such people consider their traditional structures virtually sacred and also if the tools available for modification are not yet honed to precision. In the one case we confront the unexamined life, and in the other, we propose a life not clearly defined or experienced. The dysfunctionalism of school organization today cannot wait for those ideal conditions in which change comes at leisure. We must proceed.

Plunging into organizational theory is a little like accompanying S. J. Perelman on his annual trip through the Christmas issues of *Vogue, Mademoiselle,* and *House and Garden.* One must gird oneself for the unusual and the exotic and expect a stocking stuffed with semantic gimcracks. Organizational theory proves once and for all that language is not a limitation in social-science research and discourse. The educator, untrained in the ecological balance between sociologists and management or administrative experts, can easily fall prey to the assumption that the natural habitat of all is a state of confusion. This is not true. Talcott Parsons, for example, is not obscure, but merely camouflaged. C. Wright Mills illustrated the point when he translated Parsons, Berelson, Lazarsfeld, and others for unsophisticated readers.[1] Definition will be a problem, since organizational theory or its equivalents is a product of a variety of disciplines.

Because organizational theory can be useful to the educator and because serious men have given it their full attention, we must set forth to examine it, stepping warily, senses alert, ready to risk all for a momentary glimpse of truth.

We have two immediate needs: To find a serviceable set of definitions to use in developing a rationale for school organization; and to break away from the traditional writing on educational administration, which has remained so remarkably devoid of any basic organizational theory. Management and administration are viewed here as subtopics of organization on the grounds that one cannot speculate productively on administering or managing something until one is clear what that something is, where it is supposed to go, to accomplish what, how, and when. *Management* will be used to refer to controlling behavior; *administration* will signify facilitating behavior. Not everyone will agree with these definitions, but then, not many writers in this field agree on anything.

[1]C. Wright Mills, *The Sociological Imagination,* Oxford, New York, 1959.

Let me further delimit the discussion by stating that I will not be dealing with systems theory, even though I may find myself using the word *system* occasionally. Perhaps organizational theory is a subtopic of systems theory; well and good, but that is as far as I wish to go, since systems theory may be a subtopic of some still greater universal concept. Systems theory also involves a vocabulary that may not be particularly useful to our concerns about *structure,* used in the sociological sense of the word.

Blau and Scott offer the *cui bono* (Who benefits?) system of classification of organizations, but this seems difficult to apply to schools since they most often attempt to be all things to all people, or perhaps nothing to anybody. Who it is that might benefit is not clear. Certainly the school is an organization used by many: The students, the parents, the local community, society at large, even the professionals who man its ramparts. At once, the school may benefit all of these users in different ways and degrees at different times, so the *cui bono* approach, while interesting, does not clarify matters for us.

We must also recognize that most organizational theorists have rarely examined schools in their travels; their theories have been developed in a nonschool frame of reference. I would suggest verification of this point by consulting the *Handbook of Organizations,*[2] but I sent a graduate student on that adventure once and have not heard from him since. Suffice it to say, a review of this useful volume indicates that research to verify the implementation of organizational theory in a school setting is almost nonexistent, and therefore some of the theoretical propositions offered in that volume do not hold for schools.[3] It is not clear whether this is the fault of the research or the uniqueness of schools as organizations.

Within Gouldner's framework[4] of the extremes of a ration-

[2]James G. March (ed.), *Handbook of Organizations,* Rand McNally, Chicago, 1965.
[3]See Stanley H. Udy, Jr., "The Comparative Analysis of Organizations," in ibid., pp. 6–78.
[4]Alvin W. Gouldner, "Organizational Analysis," in Robert Merton et al. (eds.), *Sociology Today,* Basic Books, New York, 1959.

al-legal model (Weber) and a natural-systems model (Comte), school organizations, particularly large units such as are found in urban areas, seem to try desperately to veer sharply toward the rational-legal extreme. While it is true that school organization tends to have semirational and functional divisions of labor with the presumption that positions are occupied according to possession of specific competencies, that is not enough. Neither is the fact that school authority, arranged in hierarchical order, is based upon both incumbency in office and presumed expertise. School organizations, it might be argued, have a central production goal, namely the servicing of a clientele to achieve the social purpose of their moral and technical socialization. If this were a clear and singular goal, it would dictate the need for precise rules of procedure to effect its accomplishment. There is the assumption by some that "the school system is responsible for a uniform product of a certain quality"[5] if it is to retain its franchise. The lack of a uniform product is profoundly evident today and is, of course, impossible to attain anyway. However, schools are *not* losing their franchise by any official decrees, and informal attacks upon them are *not* usually based upon the schools' inability to produce uniformity. Most criticism now, particularly in the inner city, is directed at what is perceived as *too much* uniformity and to the wrong model.

The rational-legal model has need for expertise at each hierarchical level in order to achieve precise production goals; hence, the traditional school argues for a teaching staff (experts) arrayed across an age-grade system of clients and directed by a corps of administrators (authority).

Examined no further, it might appear that schools are a form of bureaucracy in the classic Weberian sense. Many educators make this assertion flat out[6] and then proceed to suggest modifica-

[5]Charles E. Bidwell, "The School as a Formal Organization," in March, *Handbook of Organizations,* op. cit., p. 972.
[6]James G. Anderson, *Bureaucracy in Education,* Johns Hopkins, Baltimore, 1968; also, Daniel Levine, "Concepts of Bureaucracy in Urban School Reform," *Phi Delta Kappan,* vol. 52, no. 6, pp. 329–333, February 1971.

tions they feel are necessary to compensate for the gross dysfunctionalisms that result. The question that must be raised, however, is twofold: Are schools, urban or elsewhere, really classic bureaucracies, or even "enucleated bureaucracies"?[7] Has organizational theory been correctly used, abused, or even consulted?

> A man encountered a citizen searching the ground beneath a streetlight. "What has happened?" he asked.
>
> The citizen replied, "I lost my understanding over there in that forest."
>
> "Then why do you search for it here?" the man asked.
>
> "You fool," the citizen replied. "Can't you see that the light is better here?"

The search for understanding of the organizational problems of schools, particularly urban schools, must begin with terms that accurately describe the problem. Such terms may well dictate the range of solutions. As the fishermen of the Choco say, "The fish in the net will be the fish on the table."

Levine states categorically that urban schools "are bureaucratic institutions in the classic meaning of the term as defined by Max Weber and other nineteenth century sociologists."[8] I would say that this is not true. I would readily admit, however, that the word *bureaucracy* is carelessly used to describe any complex organization. Schools are not classic Weberian bureaucracies, and the continued assertion that they are, as a premise for any discussion, will yield no more real understanding of urban school organizational problems than the citizen will find in the convenient light of his street lamp.

Schools are quasi client-centered organizations. Their admitted dysfunctionalism occurs in part as a result of attempts to

[7]Selwyn Becker and Gerald Gordon, "An Entrepreneurial Theory of Formal Organizations," *Administrative Science Quarterly,* vol. 11, pp. 316–336, December 1966.

[8]Daniel Levine, op. cit., p. 329. With permission.

impose a bureaucratic, corporate production-oriented model upon their structure. Weber designed a bureaucracy as a rational model of efficiency for increasingly complex production-oriented organizations. He never intended bureaucracy as the ideal form for *all* kinds of organizations with multiple and diverse purposes. Without taking sides in the debate over whether education is an art or a science, it seems clear that it is not a corporate industry in which goods are produced; neither is it a monolithic structure. It is therefore inappropriate to apply to education the classic bureaucratic organizational scheme. Education, in fact, is a *process,* not a *product.* Weber did not claim that *only* bureaucracy could lay claim to rationality or the employment of competence to accomplish organizational goals. Further, bureaucracies are not the only kind of complex organizations; or reversed, all complex organizations are not bureaucracies. Put still another way, an elephant and a mouse are both mammals, have four feet, tails, two eyes, etc., but surely no one wishes to claim that elephants and mice are equivalent species. I am told that they are organized differently in many ways.

The essence of Weberian bureaucracy is rationality applied to a hierarchical structure. It is not certain that the typical American school's organizational patterns can be so described. The age-grade system, for example, has no rational defense as an educational procedure, and it is doubtful that it serves any proper educational organizational scheme. Where is it written that all ten-year-olds are sufficiently alike that they can be exposed to the same material with the expectation that the exposure will benefit all equally? Where is it written that all ten-year-olds are alike at all, and who would want them to be? At the staff level, is it a rational notion that the skills and abilities demanded of the instructional role are the same as the skills and abilities required of the managerial or administrative role? Yet we still insist on teaching experience as prerequisite to administrative licensure. The list is endless of the *customs* in education that evolved from rationalizations that are now obscure and are indefensible in their present applications.

Education is, first of all, a humanistic process: Fundamentally it involves both cognitive and affective responses from its student clients. Those clients who are undergoing the process, whom we may call the constituents of the process, are autonomous, self-interested units. They are thinking, feeling, seeing, tasting, hearing, smelling, emoting human beings. Such units inherently cannot respond to cognitive and affective stimuli in solely mechanistic ways. A product-goal process, on the other hand, selects its constituents precisely for their lack of autonomy and is thereby assured of conformity to the needs of an inanimate and predetermined product-goal. A bureaucracy is a correct scheme of organization for the impersonal routinization of a production process, but it is a dramatically incorrect choice, even an irrational one, for a humanistic process in which the necessary production controls of the constituent elements are inherently absent.

It is important to have done with further attempts to characterize schools as bureaucracies. Since it will be painful for some to discard the idea, we should provide some new definitions for examination and possible adoption. The difficulty of this task lies in the fact that schools are neither a stable nor clear-cut species of organization. The size of the school, the location (urban, suburban, small town, or rural), and the function (elementary, secondary, special purpose) are but a few of the variables that affect the definition. It seems obvious that the organizational pattern of a one-room rural school will differ sharply from that of a large-city high school. Similarly the programmatic needs of the elementary school differ from those of the high school; hence, they are organized differently. It should be just as clear that schools with culturally pluralistic populations have different needs from schools serving one-class homogeneous communities. If schools laid claim to rational organization, it seems certain that diverse purposes would have produced diverse organizational patterns to assure their accomplishment.

The diversity of purpose in schools is indisputable. Education in the United States is a *state* function; therefore, the legal framework of schools must vary in at least fifty ways. Across the nation, state laws may differ on such basic questions as who controls what, who may do what in schools, and who pays. Structurally, final authority over schools differs from state to state. There are permissive education codes and nonpermissive codes. In one, schools may do anything they wish as long as the state code does not forbid it. In the other, schools may not do anything unless the state code specifically gives them permission. In the latter case then, the state legislature has considerable power over the day-by-day operations, via enacted statutes. In the former, schools are more a product of local board control and therefore have wider latitude. Similarly, methods of collecting taxes (kinds and amounts) differ from state to state, so the lifeblood of schools is very much affected by the particular revenue policies of state or local authorities.

We must deal with such complexities as realities and be hesitant about jumping to any easy solutions. In short, we must work with a broad brush, applied tentatively.

As has been said, the school is a quasi client-centered organization. It actually has three sets of clients: Students, parents, and the community at large (which may have ethnic group, local, state, regional, or even national interests). Clearly these clients do not perceive their interests as being necessarily coterminal. To begin with, the student client is not a voluntary client; he is in school because the compulsory attendance laws demand it. If he leaves school, he is in clear and immediate danger of being judged a delinquent or social outcast.

> Young persons are compelled to enter school systems as students simply because of their placement in certain age-grades, without reference to specific performances. Furthermore, since students are to be socialized to adult life, the central activities of this role are not directly relevant to the immediate interests or lives of its incumbents. From the point of view of the student, participation in these activities is likely to

be foreign to his own preferences, yet he cannot opt for or against participation.[9]

The student client may be, in many ways, unassimilated[10] and, from the evidence of Gordon's study,[11] frequently alienated. In the inner city, such an observation is neither bold nor profound. As has been said earlier, the attempt to implement the production of a standardized Dick and Jane has had a devastating impact upon student clients who are not of the Dick and Jane culture.

Parents, the second group of clients, have still another set of expectations for schools. Broadly stated, they want the schools to help guarantee their children's success in the adult world. Social-class and ethnic-group differences in parents skew their perceptions of how this is to be accomplished. For example, the closer to the top of the socioeconomic ladder the parent is, the less dependent he is on the school; the upper classes may see the school's role as supplementary, while in contrast, the lower classes may view the school as an all-important gatekeeper. It is the difference between reassurance and assurance.

The poor do not have the resources to compensate for the failures of the school. They must depend upon the school to do its job. Parental bitterness in the inner city reflects this knowledge and the frustration and anger that result when their hopes are unfulfilled. Middle- and upper-class parents can offset school failures, but they are usually more anxious about "wasted" tax money or the potential loss of the competitive advantage their children must maintain. They do tend, however, to understand the crucial role of education in the social system better than do parents who must concern themselves first with economic survival.

Parents then represent a wide range of possible client

[9]Charles E. Bidwell, op. cit., p. 973. With permission.
[10]Ibid., p. 991.
[11]C. W. Gordon, *The Social System of the High School,* Free Press, Glencoe, Ill., 1957.

responses to which schools must be acutely sensitive, or at least it may be so alleged. Confronted with too many stimulating encounters with parents, schools may, and often do, retreat behind either organizational or professional defenses and then exclude the parents as clients, except when those parents promise faithfully to play only supporting roles. Most educators in the field publicly decry such exclusion, but will vote for it without hesitation because it is a matter of what they perceive to be their own survival. It has never been clearly defined what organizational role parents should play in the activities of schools, since most schools are not sure of differences between client and patron relationships. In situations where schools claim *in loco parentis* privileges over children, the parents are surely clients, but in a system such as the one that proposes the use of vouchers, the parent would become a patron or customer. Organizational responses must discriminate between these two parental roles.

It is the society as client that has imposed the most unequal, and perhaps impossible, demands upon the school. The school must be, at once and on demand, a primary socialization agent (values, attitudes, etc.), a trainer (skills, understandings), a social service agent, a recreation group, a community center, a health agent, and a provider of a host of other functions. In the urban setting, with its incredible diversity, the range of expectations and demands may seem limitless to harried educators. It is little wonder that some educators hastily retreat behind whatever organizational barriers they can erect. It is this defensive posture, often perceived by outsiders as an impersonal run around, that suggests the pejorative term *bureaucracy*. Commonly, bureaucracy means a complex organization that seems unresponsive to specific people with specific needs at specific times. In short, a school is an organization trying to do too many things for too many different kinds of clients, most of whom are, at one time or another, dissatisfied, and some of whom never asked for the service in the first place.

The larger the number of student clients, the greater the

need to impose ordered procedures to service them. The greater the number of tasks to be performed, the greater the need for some kind of organized system. Remarkably, schools with varying clients with varying needs historically evolved organizational forms that were adopted across the land without any apparent regard for either these clients or the differences in their needs. Teachers were allocated a loosely defined instructional role that assumed a certain kind and amount of expert training, though both the kind and the amount differ from state to state and even from community to community within states. Organizational responses to the wide variance in role definition or to the realities of the actual inhabitants of such roles should be varied. A teacher with a bare two years of college or normal-school training can fill one kind of status, while a five-year-program graduate may be able to fulfill other expectations. The fact of being a generalist or a specialist in content implies still other organizational options. The elementary specialist (music, art, etc.) is often cast in a role of a wandering player, but the same specialist in a high school setting is stationary. Administrators were given managerial roles without managerial training[12] and expected to play administrative roles simultaneously. A classic role conflict came when the principal was continually expected to make employment decisions about teachers (managerial role) at the same time that he was expected to be the confidante, helper, and consultant to those same teachers (administrative role). Some outriders have suggested that principals should probably be trained in schools of management or in public administration, but not in schools of education, in the same way that hospital administrators are not trained in medical schools. Actually, in most states schools are legally supposed to be the responsibility of an elected board of citizens with professional personnel to implement board policy. However, the organization of professionals, both administrator-managers and teachers, soon produced a professional-dominated system.

[12]Recall that I am using the term *managerial* to signify controlling activities, and the term *administrative* to mean facilitating activities.

The assumption of a professional is that he is entitled to significant autonomy in the performance of his tasks. Further, "specialization of professional tasks lead[s] to structural patterns of autonomy."[13] Of course, the more professional autonomy there is, the less bureaucracy is possible. Even hierarchical authority may be weakened as professionals at every stratum exert their individual wills and worship their particular gods. Is the educator to be loyal first to his school, or to his professional organization (teachers' association), or to his union? Negotiated contracts are now becoming a severe restriction on how any school organization may respond, for as more and more tasks are defined in detail in binding contracts, variant behavior is discouraged or forbidden, which inhibits both the organization and the exercise of professional autonomy. Militant teacher organizations, working solely in behalf of their memberships' salary interests and working conditions, often make organizational change a near impossibility. Maybe citizen boards can now hope only to contain the system rather than control it. Secretaries of defense have been known to have some similar problems with the professional military.

Etzioni attempted to describe schools using his compliance variable as the central classification: "Compliance is a relationship consisting of power employed by superiors to control subordinates and the orientation of subordinates to this power."[14] By now, he has probably realized that the distribution of power in schools is unpredictable: The expert teacher is often not expert and may have varying degrees of autonomy; the manager is an administrator, or the administrator is a manager; the citizen board does or does not make policy; different actors in the organization change roles as organizational functions change; or the informal organiza-

---

[13]Fred E. Katz, "The School as a Complex Organization: A Consideration of Patterns of Autonomy," *Harvard Educational Review,* vol. 34, no. 3, pp. 428–455, 1964.

[14]Amitai Etzioni, *A Comparative Analysis of Complex Organizations,* Free Press, New York, 1961, p. xv.

tions of teachers and other personnel within schools are persuasive. Besides, the student clients have decided to go their own way anyway. The distraught researcher can find little that will hold still to either lower-, middle-, or upper-range theory. Katz started with autonomy as the flipside of compliance and ran into the same problems of inconsistency.[15] Bidwell tried a straightforward descriptive statement that included many of the contradictions, conflicts, and cross-purposes. In so doing, he acknowledged that schools did not fit any particular working theoretical model, and he retreated to the term *framework* as sufficient.[16] Gross concurs when he cautions:

> Implicit in discussions . . . of the organizational structure of the school are two assumptions that deserve empirical examination. The first is that there is basic agreement on the organizational objective of the schools. The second is that there is agreement on the rights and obligations associated with the various positions in education. Sociological analysis suggests that both assumptions may in fact be tenuous in many school systems, and that lack of agreement on educational objectives and role definitions may constitute major dysfunctional elements in the functioning of the school . . .[17]

It was Comte's conviction that the "final order which arises spontaneously is always superior to that which human combination had, by anticipation, constructed."[18] Certainly school organization has indeed risen "spontaneously," some might even say haphazardly. The age-grade system emerged from the one-room rural schoolhouse, as did the long summer harvest vacation. The former seemed functional for small numbers, and the latter was an

[15]Katz, loc. cit.
[16]Bidwell, op. cit., pp. 972–1018.
[17]Neal Gross, "Some Contributions of Sociology to the Field of Education," *Harvard Educational Review,* vol 29, no. 4, p. 276, Fall 1959. With permission.
[18]Auguste Comte, *Early Essays on Social Philosophy* (H. D. Hutton, trans.), George Routledge & Sons, Ltd, London, n. d., p. 325.

economic necessity for both teachers and pupils. Similarly, the selection of a first or principal teacher as nominal head of the school became necessary as school sizes increased and the need for coordination and management became evident. Principal teacher became simply *principal,* and now, in some places, the incumbent insists upon the title *administrator,* although his role definition is still unclear. When schools continued to grow and multiply into larger districts and systems, additional positions were added as functional needs seemed appropriate. The superstructure of administration that now encrusts education seemed to follow Parkinson's laws or, more often, simply grew without any overall organizational rationale. Trying to analyze and classify what happened is a latter-day development. Thus school organization, as it presently manifests itself, is like an old house on which succeeding generations have been building quaint additions here and there, now and then, to meet peculiar needs. It has no rhythm or style now, but it has a certain nostalgic charm, a comfortable lived in quality that some of its inhabitants are prone to defend with steadfast resolution. It is also the despair of others who see its destructiveness and dysfunctionalism. Following a newer vision, they want a major remodeling, some even a razing, in order to begin anew.

The school thus became a complex organization, trying to fulfill many functions and promises. It was a formal organization because it was sanctioned by law and governed in part by codified regulations. Because of the school's clients with their pursuit of a thousand special interests and purposes, its tempo of development and the unique structures it had to create, the school became perhaps a *singular organizational form.* The school could be called a natural-systems model. That classification is sufficiently imprecise, a tent to cover all manner of wondrous things. It is also possible that the school, in all its forms and functions, is not one thing, but rather a number of organizational structures trying to operate compatibly in the same space and at the same time.

Thus far I have made both descriptive and argumentative

statements and reviewed their possible relationships with organizational theories. I have generalized about some things that schools are not, which can lead us to at least one proposition: *Schools are either derivative of a natural-systems model or they are multiple models operating simultaneously.* Perhaps we have begun to evolve a theoretical position.

But before we proceed down this road, let me file a few notes on theory itself. Starting with a theory and then searching out the facts to substantiate it can be Procrustean: A person can be sorely tempted to stretch some facts to fit his model, or he may be persuaded to lop off those facts that hang over the edges. Either way, he may lose something vital and important. Perhaps it is better to start with the facts or the concepts that have some reasonable hope of validation and then seek some explanation of how these facts or concepts relate to one another. Each such explanation becomes an hypothesis, subject to some kind of empirical verification. If the hypothesis is verified time and time again in replicated studies, then the theory is pretty good. If nothing new comes along (new facts or observations or a new explanation of relationship) and the theory seems to be consistently predictive, it just may be a law or principle. By predictive, I mean that the application of the theory in new circumstances predicts certain results and those results regularly occur.

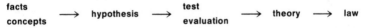

facts
concepts $\longrightarrow$ **hypothesis** $\longrightarrow$ **test evaluation** $\longrightarrow$ **theory** $\longrightarrow$ **law**

Thompson suggests that in dealing with organizational theory, we may use a *closed-system strategy* or an *open-system strategy.*[19] He goes on:

> If, instead of assuming cloture, we assume that a system contains more variables than we can comprehend at one time or predict, we must resort to a different sort of logic. We can, if we

[19]James D. Thompson, *Organizations in Action,* McGraw-Hill, New York, 1967, p. 4. With permission.

wish, assume that the system is determinate by nature, but that it is our incomplete understanding which forces us to expect surprise or the intrusion of uncertainty. In this case we can employ a natural-system model (open system) . . .

A second version of the natural-system approach . . . views the organization as a unit in interaction with its environment . . . it is clear that in contrast to the rational model approach, this research area focuses on variables not subject to complete control by the organization and hence not contained within a closed system of logic. It is also clear that students (of this approach) regard interdependence of organization and environment as inevitable or natural, and as adaptive or functional.[20]

Once again, the school qualifies as an open system because of its historical interdependence with its environment, which, in turn, contains a host of variables that remain uncontrolled by the school. Again, bureaucracy is shown to be an inappropriate closed-system model. What we often encounter in school organizational problems is a choice between rich theories evolved from few or no facts and mountains of facts left unorganized by any theory. There is a reasonable explanation for this phenomenon, at least in the educational world.

As has been said, educators have tended to assume schools were bureaucracies, a closed-system approach. Committed to this point, they have attempted to develop all manner of generalizations useful to their administrative theories, but not useful to consideration of any other organizational theory. They implicitly accept the existence of an organizational theory (bureaucracy). The incredible tonnage of data collected may or may not be useful, depending upon the validity of the organizational theory. Levine,[21] for example, cites "institutional complexity and overload" as major

[20]Ibid., pp. 6–7. With permission.
[21]Daniel Levine, "Concepts of Bureaucracy in Urban School Reform," *Phi Delta Kappan,* vol. 52, no. 6, p. 329, February 1971.

problems of urban schools. He describes these as "the tendency for institutions to be ineffective when their internal structures are too complicated to allow for adequate communications, or when the external frameworks in which they function are rendered inoperable by having too large a burden placed on them."[22] We cannot be sure whether he means *organizations* or *institutions;* they are not the same. *Institution* is a much broader term and generally refers simply to normative patterns of behavior or action, but it is doubtful if the term is precisely useful to complex organizations, which, in fact, could be one kind of institution. Neither are we clear about what *external frameworks* may be. Regardless, the discussion of complexity and overload that follows is premised upon the assumption that urban schools are classic bureaucracies, and whatever facts or arguments submitted are molded to that construct. Since that assumption is incorrect, then what follows is superfluous. Anderson[23] similarly makes the bureaucratic argument, tests it with instruments, and verifies that his premise of bureaucratic administration is valid. Of course, he started with the assumption that schools were bureaucracies. Recalling the elephant and the mouse, this is like assuming that all mammals are elephants, and then proving that because mice walk on four legs, use their two eyes and ears, reproduce, and display a host of other elephantlike behaviors, they should be classified as elephants. Had Anderson started with a different organizational theory and its derivative vocabulary, it is possible he would have validated a quite different administrative theory.

Thompson suggests that in attempting to understand complex organizations, we remember that "this is a broad if still shallow field."[24] It follows then that administrative theory and management theory constructed without recourse to a foundational

[22]Ibid.
[23]James G. Anderson, *Bureaucracy in Education*, Johns Hopkins, Baltimore, 1968.
[24]Thompson, loc. cit.

organizational theory must be even more unsubstantial. Possibly a grand exchange of ideas by an interdisciplinary team of organizational theorists, management theorists, and administrative theorists, guided by the architectural principle that form should follow function, would result in the fattening of each's field and finally the development of a working model of an appropriate school organization. Certainly, schools need the attention of such theorists, particularly those interested in testing their ideas within a living, breathing, desperately functioning, natural system. Empirical verification should, of course, follow close on the heels of such investigations.

Confronting the problem of organization from the less theoretical perspective of the schoolman, the initial question is: What needs to be organized? That, of course, depends upon a prior value decision about what one wants to accomplish. If, for example, we were to accept the need to establish multicultural education in this democratic and pluralistic society (see Chapter Three), then we would have an imposing set of purposes to implement. If we further were to accept the sublime intent to individualize education as much as possible, we would have both another purpose and a process as well. Let us assume, for the sake of argument, that these have become our foremost educational purposes. Social-service purposes, or other noneducational purposes, will be considered later.

We must organize *people*. The people of education are, of course, the students, the educators, and the participating members of the community. The present age-grade organization would, naturally, be inappropriate, since any typical heterogeneous student population scheduled to receive individualized instruction could not respond to age-grade compartmentalization based on the irrelevant criteria of chronological age and years in school. Grouping of students would have to be designed to provide freedom of response to individual educational needs. The normal wide range of student needs would also dictate an allocation of teachers using criteria more associated with expertise in content than in some hypothetical structural skill (a sixth-*grade* teacher, for example, as opposed to the more appropriate science specialist). There would be a similar allocation of facilitators (administrators) and some kind of management or control center, perhaps manned by a group of students, teachers, administrators, and community representatives, who in turn would be responsible to a higher district authority. Certainly the typical hierarchial structure would be out of place. The control center would have to be at least semiautonomous in terms of internal, at hand, educational decisions. Noneducational decisions would be subject to a noneducational organizational pattern.

Secondly, we must organize *ideas*. Clearly, knowledge and the processes of discovering it have a structure.[25] Knowledge is not static; it constantly evolves, grows, and challenges us to new discoveries. Therefore, the organization of knowledge in schools cannot be static. For the learners, also changing constantly in response to an ever-changing environment, knowledge comes in a constant process of experiencing stimuli and reorganizing personal classification systems. The current popular outcry for relevance in content may be so much flapdoodle. First, there is little in human experience that is equally relevant to all. Secondly, individualized instruction precludes any universal definition of relevance. However, there is a clear principle of starting from the known (reality) and exploring the unknown as it extends from that reality. One may suspect then that complaining students mean "realness" rather than relevance. Thus the organization of ideas starts with reality and moves through an evolving structure, probably inductively, until each individual, at his own level, not only possesses his personal version of certain standard skills, abilities, and assorted useful facts, but he has also mastered the methods of discovery, analysis, and creative thought that will enable him to solve problems he has not yet confronted, as well as some that have not yet been defined.

Finally, we must organize *things*. The things of education are inanimate; they are the spatial environment for learning and the

[25]Jerome S. Bruner, *The Process of Education,* Harvard, Cambridge, Mass., 1961, pp. 17–32.

equipment, such as the furniture, the machines, and the books. Selection and organization of the things can have a profound impact on the organization of either the people or the ideas. The self-contained classroom, for example, represents a philosophy of education and an environment designed for an allocated age-grade population of students and a teacher. If the grouping definition changes and the approach to knowledge changes, then the definitions of space, such as what constitutes a classroom, are subject to change. Individualization implies a term like *learning centers* where the population is never constant.

Furniture built to stand in rows says a great deal about how much the school is committed to individualization and flexibility in dealing with content. We are reminded by the architects again of the principle that form follows function; thus our organization of things must conform to our decisions on function. In education, function evolves and changes. The forms must therefore have sufficient flexibility to adjust to those thousand visions and revisions.

Three factors that have been deterrents to school reorganization are the unyielding conventions involving time, space, and role definition. Considering schools as open systems with multiple goals, none of these three factors has to be held constant anymore. There are many possibilities that rethinking of the use of time and space and role definition might suggest.

Time presently fixes the beginning and the ending of the learner's school day, which usually coincides with the commercial workday. Time also parcels out the learner's experience within that day, i.e., so many minutes to learn this and so many minutes to learn that, which would conceivably be defensible if school were a production system. It is possible to use time as an ally instead of a constraint; nothing in educational research indicates that learning must or can only take place during certain hours or in given segments of those hours. In other words, school could start as early as six o'clock or seven o'clock in the morning (day-care centers sometimes do if they want to adequately serve their clientele), if that were appropriate. Similarly, school could operate well into the evening (as adult-education schools do now), if that were necessary for the learners. With computer assistance and with the use of time modules of shorter duration than the usual period, an almost infinite number of combinations could be constructed to serve each student's particular need as well as to serve large-group instruction, small-group instruction, tutorials, and independent study. Such scheduling would also offer the possibilities of a wider range of both organized and independent learning experiences, and the flexibility introduced by the ease with which the computer can handle such complexity means that scheduling and rescheduling could be almost a daily affair. Students who wanted to work could come at times suited to their employment, and they could even be joined by their parents if desired, since fixing the time in a person's life during which he may receive instruction (ages seven to seventeen, for example) really makes no sense at all.

Place need not be fixed. Education is a process, not a place, as the growing number of "schools without walls" are demonstrating. Learning, particularly in the multistimuli urban setting, can take place almost anywhere, with the advantage that out-of-school experiences often have a greater ring of reality than in-school experiences. Learning can take place both in and out of school, as schools have recognized for years with their elaborate arrangements for excursions or trips out and their importation of resources into the school. Within the school, given the abandonment of the production-system–self-contained classroom in an age-graded sequence, the student could move about among learning centers as the need arose. Experimental schools today have already demonstrated the practicality of individual student carrels or "offices" that act as home bases for the learners. Architects and environmental designers have moved a long way toward flexible space in both elementary and secondary schools.[26]

Role definition is similarly open to transformation. When

[26]The reader is urged to see the Architecture and Education issue of the *Harvard Educational Review,* vol. 39, no. 4, 1969, with particular attention to the material by Maurice Smith and Robert Goodman.

the age-grade system is relinquished, teachers automatically become something other than mere custodians of certain age groups and fixed portions of content. At the elementary level, they can become specialists, as their colleagues in art and music already are, but without the constraints of trying to decide whether a drawing or a sculpture is of fifth- or sixth-grade quality. I remember an absurdity that seemed ultimate: A college instructor, asked to evaluate a poem, called it "a good piece of undergraduate writing." Some teachers might consider that their instructional role is best played in large-group sessions, while others might find their strength is a tutorial or the direction of an independent-study project. The need for hierarchial arrangements in which someone is the boss quickly erodes in such a program, and administrators can really become expediters and facilitators. The management role is exercised by an emergent group of students, teachers, administrators, and even community people, acting as a kind of board of directors. Such organization would be experimental; it would need to evolve from experience. Present school administration, often most concerned with management, i.e., control and maintenance, emerges as a distinctively antiexperimental force. It would have to be displaced.

In Lloyd K. Bishop's useful book, he advocates what he calls "the organic-adaptive system,"[27] but his plan includes many activities that are only related to the educational process, not directly a part of it. It may be that these activities are better served by alternative organizations, and their inclusion in the educational model, as was the case in the past, would be inappropriate and debilitating. The theoretical conceptions underlying any designing of change are well documented and discussed in Bennis, Benne, and Chin's book *The Planning of Change*,[28] a volume that any educational sociologist must have in his library.

As has been stated, the school is asked to perform many

[27]Lloyd K. Bishop, *Individualizing Educational Systems,* Harper & Row, New York, 1971.
[28]Warren G. Binnis, Kenneth D. Benne, and Robert Chin, *The Planning of Change,* 2d ed., Holt, New York, 1969.

functions that are ancillary rather than directly educational. Some of these activities are directly supportive of the educational program (although not educational in themselves), and others seem totally detached. It would seem logical that these auxiliary activities not interfere with the primary educational purpose of the school. Structurally then, they should be apart, and organized in forms appropriate for whatever their particular purpose might be, for example, independent service modules. Structural overlap could occur, but *never* at the expense of educational concerns. Child-welfare services, for example, are important supportive activities, but they are not efficiently performed by educational experts (teachers and principals), though such personnel may need to be consulted along the way. The nature of child-welfare services implies a different kind of expertise than educational personnel possess and therefore a different organizational structure to accomplish its important ends. The same might be said of the many other noneducational activities demanded of the school, such as the use of schoolchildren as a cheap communication channel to parents as taxpayers or as community members.

When diverse functions are rationalized into one single organizational structure, conflict, inefficiency, and profound dysfunctionalism occur. In addition, when each of these functions in itself involves ever-changing responses, the result can be the chaos found in many urban schools. Under such conditions, if management does not want to face the dilemmas of the proverbial one-armed paperhanger, it is often forced to see its function as one of standardizing responses (an inappropriate response to diverse needs). The solution, organizationally, is to diversify the internal structures or to separate the functions and create appropriate organizations for each.

In summary, organizational theory is still in its formative stages. Although it should be the antecedent base for administrative and management theory, in education the reverse has often been true. When this is the case, the language of organizational theory may be imprecise (since it is also derivative of many disciplines and perspectives) and confusing. The analysis of the school as an organization has suffered because (1) educational administrative theory preceded organizational theory and has dominated all considerations of structure; (2) organizational theory has been couched in language unfamiliar to educators, and the educators, not seeing themselves in it, abandoned it; and (3) organizational theorists, for the most part, have used organizations other than schools for their theory-building and research settings.

Schools, educationally speaking, are probably open systems. When they attempt to absorb incompatible functions (non-educational) into one structure (often misperceived as a closed bureaucratic system), they have loaded stresses on the school structure that are apparently beyond its capacity to sustain. The clear need in school organization is to reorganize and to do so with the help of, first, organizational theorists, and then, management and administrative theorists. Of course, the educators must be willing and able to *listen* and *inform* their benefactors. Perhaps an educational sociologist will be drafted to serve as moderator and interpreter of these complex negotiations.

chapter five

the role of
the community
in education

American democracy, traditionally, has been suspicious of any power but the power of its people expressed in consensus. Even though interdependence forced the urban dweller to seek governmental intervention to protect him from exploitation, at no time did he consciously consent to the unchecked usurpation of power by the government of any elite. The individual citizen wanted protection, but it was the assurance of his individuality, and the retention of his civil, economic, and social rights that he wanted most. He accepted government as a necessity, but it had to be *his* government ("the consent of the governed"), and he had to feel that he had direct participation in it and, in his individual way, control over it. Perhaps his participation and control was to be eventually expressed through groups, i.e., organized interest groups, voluntary associations, and the like. Whatever the mechanism, the right to participate and the assurance of control, no matter how abstract, had to be there.

The issue of community participation and/or community control of schools has become an incendiary issue, particularly in urban schools, because a great many people have discovered that they have lost control of their schools and that they no longer participate in the education process. Their sense of direct, intimate, and participatory government has been offended, even upended, by the evident depersonalization of, and sometimes oppression by, large urban school districts.

> It is true that schools, under law, belong to the people, and that most urban school boards and systems seem to have forgotten this. It is also true that schools, under law, do not belong just to parents, or students, or the power structure of the community, but to the *total* public, who is required by law (1) to support schools by paying universal local property taxes, plus pertinent state and federal taxes, and (2) to select school board members and vote on tax rates and bond issues [in most states].
>
> A school board, therefore, is an *elected* group of citizens [in most states], charged with the responsibility of governing a school district, *in behalf* of that general public. Such a board is *accountable* to that public and may be scrutinized by the public, or any segment thereof, at any time, to review its stewardship in carrying out the sole purpose for its existence, i.e. providing of quality education for all children within its jurisdiction, relentlessly, and without diversion to other purposes or priorities.[1]

[1]Donald R. Thomas, "Urban School Boards: The Need for Accountability," *Education and Urban Society,* vol. 1, no. 3, p. 289, May 1969. By permission of the publisher, Sage Publications, Inc.

In small towns and in suburbia, this arrangement usually works. As Kenneth Clark points out:

> Community control of schools is a given in many of the towns, smaller cities, and suburbs of the nation. If an epidemic of low academic achievement swept over these schools, drastic measures would be imposed. Administrators and school boards would topple, and teachers would be trained or dismissed. If students were regularly demeaned and dehumanized in those schools, cries of outrage in the P.T.A.'s would be heard—and listened to—and action to remove the offending personnel would be taken immediately. Accountability is so implicit a given that the term "community control" never is used by those who have it.[2]

If the smaller-sized unit seems to achieve accountability because citizens feel or know they can both control and participate in school decision-making, then the urban problem could be quickly resolved by the simple solution of decentralization or the division of the large district into smaller, autonomous units. In essence, this was what was proposed for New York City by the Bundy report.[3] New York City, however, discovered that this solution was not enough. There were a myriad of other problems to be solved. One may suspect that the New York formula turned out to be both a blessing and a curse when other cities confronted the same tensions and demands. New York City is unique in some very significant ways (for example, its board is uniquely bound to the municipal political structure), yet the powerful molders of opinion who live there and write endlessly on politics and social and economic problems seem to feel that any solution proposed for New York simply must have a universal application. The Bundy report plowed much valuable ground and

[2]Kenneth Clark, in the introduction to Mario Fantini, Marilyn Gittell, and Richard Magat, *Community Control and the Urban School,* Praeger, New York, 1970, pp. ix–x. With permission.
[3]Fantini et al., ibid., p. 100.

unearthed a wide variety of other issues that were embedded in the simplistic phrase *community control.* While the report was a service to the country, any continued insistence that New York's problems are the nation's problems distracts attention from serious work in other cities.

The counterforce to decentralization is a growing advocacy of *metropolitanism.* Urbanologists who examine the problems of law enforcement, transportation, welfare, housing, health care, and sewers, to name a few, see more adequate solutions in the establishment of metropolitan government and regional planning. Certainly the interdependence of the central city and the suburbs calls for increased coordination among these units, particularly when the central city seems to be experiencing the worst of the problems and cannot find solutions without extensive suburban cooperation. It is now evident that education too may need to go the route of metropolitanism in order to achieve increased fiscal efficiency and integration and to obtain true cultural pluralism. I have advocated elsewhere the creation of metropolitan educational authorities.

> A Metropolitan Educational Authority could be a Board of 12 to 15 people who employed their own professional research and evaluation staff. The territory governed by such a Board would then be divided into sub-areas, each with its own citizen advisory board and a chief administrator whose tenure would be subject to continued high performance ratings. Within the Authority, there would be specialty schools and activities which cut across sub-area jurisdictions.[4]

The Richmond, Virginia, case in which a federal judge

---

[4]Donald R. Thomas, "The Scene Has Changed and the Time Is Now," *Needs of Elementary and Secondary Education for the Seventies: A Compendium of Policy Papers,* Committee on Education and Labor, General Subcommittee on Education, House of Representatives, 91st Cong., Washington, D.C., 1970, p. 749.

ordered the unification of the virtually all-black Richmond city schools with the virtually all-white surrounding two counties was significant because it challenged the use of school-district boundaries (a creation of the state) as a method of exclusion or segregation. An earlier Detroit decision used the same reasoning. If segregationists had envisioned abandoning the cities to minority groups with the view that district boundaries would protect them, these decisions made achievement of the vision impossible. Metropolitan school districts now loom as distinct possibilities for future school organization. I would simply add that such districts still need semiautonomous subdistricts with which local groups can readily identify, providing, of course, that such subdistricts assure integration.

It is necessary then to solve the problem of school jurisdictional areas in a way that does not set up political, social, and economic distinctions that, in turn, cause inequality of opportunity for children. At the same time, it seems foolish to ignore the tradition and the values of significant community participation in the educational process. When autonomous community control, in the pattern of the towns, smaller cities, and suburbs is applied to the metropolitan area, it seems to defeat the higher priority goals of integration, cultural pluralism, and metropolitan coordination. The drive for such control arises primarily out of the frustration of black ghetto inhabitants "who now despair of ever accomplishing significant changes in the dismal education scene their children experience."[5] It is also based upon certain assumptions, which David K. Cohen states are:

> . . . by no means self-evident: a) that liberal programs of educational reform were in fact tried on a significant scale; b) that where they were tried, they failed; or c) that political and administrative change is necessarily a precondition for change in the distribution of educational achievement.[6]

[5]Thomas, "Urban School Boards," p. 289.
[6]David K. Cohen, "The Price of Community Control," *Commentary,* vol. 48, no. 1, p. 23, July 1969. With permission. Copyright © by the American Jewish Committee.

Reform has not taken place on a significant scale. Although integration in the South is now reaching a level of significance, efforts toward it are declining in the rest of the country. Reforms that were to be the cornerstones of the Elementary and Secondary Education Act of 1965 were never insisted upon and consequently were never widespread. Significant change is never likely to occur rapidly, but Americans, particularly leaders who must achieve results in order to remain leaders, are notoriously impatient. Pressure began with what some have called the revolution of rising expectations, spawned in the civil-rights movement and in the early community-action programs of the Office of Economic Opportunity. The former envisioned equality at last, and the latter began to prove that local community initiative could, in fact, be a powerful tool for the achievement of self-determination. Both were legitimate dreams, but the power structures in a racist society were resistant (as was to be expected), and progress has been slower for many than they could possibly endure.

> A policy of institutional reform clearly could not depend for its mandate only on the support of the institutions to be reformed, however powerful their influence. Mayors, school superintendents, public-spirited bankers, representatives of organized labor, pastors of churches, were not the accredited spokesmen of the poor. They stood rather for that established power whose rivalries and mutual accommondations had always vitiated the good faith of the concern they expressed. Some countervailing authority was needed to protect the programs against the encroachment of institutional self-interest upon genuine service.[7]

If there is any evidence that political and administrative change is, indeed, a precondition for any real educational change, it lies in the reaction of the power structures to the poverty and minority

[7]Peter Marris and Martin Rein, *Dilemmas of Social Reform,* Atherton, New York, 1967, p. 164. With permission.

communities' thrust for equality and fair play. Politicians recognized in community self-determination the inherent threat to their own crude self-interest and reacted swiftly to demolish the antipoverty programs, particularly those generated by community action. Mayors and governors insisted upon the right to veto all such programs, and the record is clear that they exercised that veto right regularly. School superintendents too insisted that all school-reform programs be directed by themselves or their subordinates with the obvious result that reform was at best minimal, and never at the expense of the power of the Establishment. Even teachers sought to protect their working conditions and status arrangements, bargaining for their own maintenance as higher in priority than reforms that would enhance educational equality for children. Business interests tended to see reform in almost purely economic terms. Arrangements with schools to supply materials and services were not to be threatened by restructuring of jurisdictions or power, and the tax rate was not to be disturbed.

> For some of the members at least, the corporation represents a value-laden institution that outranks the local community as a focus of loyalty and a medium for self-realization. It would scarcely be saying too much and perhaps is tritely apparent that people may be more citizens of the corporations for whom they work than of the local communities in which they reside.[8]

It was no wonder then that poverty communities in general, and the militant black communities in particular, began to think about the *colony theory.*

> To use their own language, they want to stop being colonies. They want their dependence on the benevolence of ruling

[8]Norton Long, "The Corporation, Its Satellites, and the Local Community," in David W. Minar and Scott Greer (eds.), *The Concept of Community,* Aldine, Chicago, 1969, p. 163. With permission.

outsiders (most of whom, in any case, are not very benevolent) to cease. And they will not be mollified by provisions for a few of their number—by adopting its speech and behavior patterns, and by agreeing to be instruments of its institutions—to enter that class.[9]

The Congress of Racial Equality (CORE) has been perhaps the most outspoken advocate of not only black self-determination and participation, but also outright separatism and what they define as nationalism. CORE sees the primary problem of black people as being powerlessness. They insist that without power to resist racism and oppression, blacks can only be considered slaves. Separation, they argue, defines the relationship between persons occupying two pieces of land. Each group controls all of the social, political, and economic institutions in its given area; each group controls the flow of goods and services in its area; and each group controls the perpetuation of its particular lifestyle, the creation of values and norms, and the continuation of traditions and the evolution of law. Separatism means community control, perpetuation of one's lifestyle and group heritage, and maximization of one's interests. The validity of CORE's argument that racism and classism have rendered most blacks powerless is, of course, undeniable. But that a culturally pluralistic democracy could endure the separatism of each and every group that saw itself as having a separate lifestyle and group heritage is indeed questionable. It may also be self-evident that power needs to be redistributed, but whether or not the erection of autonomous islands of power, almost as in the manner of separate sovereign nations, is valid is disputable.

Community participation and control is technically a reality. School districts in most of the United States are ruled by elected representatives of the people. The breakdown of this repre-

[9]Alan A. Altshuler, *Community Control: The Black Demand for Participation in Large American Cities,* Pegasus (Western), New York, 1970, p. 15. With permission.

sentative democratic system comes when the size of the electoral body is so large that the various individual factions' legitimate interests are lost. Power is certainly a function of a group's access to information about what is happening in the school district. In the large city district, few people have access to information, partly because the control center can refuse to release information that might cause a shift in power and a consequent loss of control. Power is also a function of access to resources that enable the holder of those resources to utilize them for his own ends. Few people have sufficient resources to campaign widely for election to the board of control (school board, board of trustees, etc.). Put another way, power is a function of the ability to restrict access to information and resources. This is particularly true in large cities because the required information is more complex and because greater resources are needed to successfully invade a whole city's locus of control.

If school boards were to be elected by wards or other subareas, blacks could achieve representation, but in most cities they would still be a minority. They could therefore argue that someone else was still controlling them. If that *someone else* is generalized to mean *whites,* then, of course, there is no solution but complete autonomy for blacks, and we return to the ensuing problems of separatism.

If school boards are elected at large, then each candidate needs greater resources and a more significant power base among voters. Historically, this arrangement has tended to favor wealthy candidates with strong ties to the current Establishment. Again, blacks or other minority groups may feel powerless in the face of such odds. However, so does any group, white, black, or brown, that tries to assault the power structure to achieve change. The answer, traditionally, in American politics has been the formation of alliances that pledge mutual support and, if elected, a sharing of power. It seems unlikely that this tradition will soon be discarded.

Democracy is not universally respected in America. Men

of power are frequently impatient with its slow, perhaps inefficient, ways. If such men emerge from corporations, where democracy is neither a requirement nor a value, they can become annoyed with the need for consultation or the average man on the street's participation in the decision-making process. To them, this procedure seems wasteful and inefficient. Thomas Vail, editor and publisher of the *Cleveland Plain Dealer,* the largest newspaper in Ohio, once wrote of his city and its control:

> . . . The sad fact is that Cleveland really has no effective establishment. This is one of our major local problems. The "old families" who founded this community from success in minerals, steel and heavy industry once were an establishment which had economic, political and social power . . .

> However, the founding families have through the generations split their fortunes among heirs, diluting their influence. In addition, few families have ever produced ability in every generation. The progeny of these original rich are now found on boards of hospitals, museums, schools, colleges and the like . . .

> In the old days this establishment met and decided important local and national matters at the Union Club. Today at the Union Club, many of the names are the same but the power is gone. Another and different "establishment" might be our captains of industry and their lawyers and accountants who serve them. These are the "number one men" or chief executive officers of our leading firms. They operate and control the Greater Cleveland Growth Association [Chamber of Commerce]. . . .

> [But] Cleveland does not have a group of oil men like Houston, auto men like Detroit or steel men like Pittsburgh. There is no hierarchial group which can call the tune and force everyone else to fall in line.

> . . . The only possibility that exists for leadership in Cleveland is the emergence of a personality with a power base who can

somehow gain such respect from our private and public men that he will be listened to and followed . . .[10]

What Vail is really posing as an issue is Establishment control versus people control, autocracy versus democracy. It seems tiresome to have to repeat all the clichés that have been held sacred to democracy these nearly 200 years of America's existence, but we must remind ourselves of our authentic American revolutionary élan and the principles upon which it is based, not so that we can pay lip service to such principles, but so that we can reassert in actions our determination to make them operative. Blacks and other minority groups, the general poor, and even our youth can rightfully challenge us, out of their experiences, either to live democracy or to abandon it for some other arrangement yet unrefined.

Separatism as a form of community control implies the abandonment of hope for democracy, and it is certainly inimical to the achievement of a peace that is multicultural, multiracial, and multisocial class. While CORE might argue that separatism would at least promote mutual respect based upon equal power, the price may be too great for the nation, and there may be other ways to accomplish the same goals. It has been said of John Dewey's educational philosophy not that it was tried and found wanting, but rather that it was not tried at all because for many it was too difficult. The same might be said of democracy.

The argument that separatism is the only way by which a group can attain its identity seems similarly deficient. If all groups so reasoned, and who is to say that all groups do not have an equal right to make such a claim, the result would be chaos. The converse question is, of course, can a racial or ethnic group attain identity without separatism? My answer must be positive if a full trial of multicultural, multiracial education is achieved and small, direct, participatory units of government are established. By *full trial,* I mean

[10]Thomas Vail, "Establishment Has No Power," publisher's column, *Cleveland Plain Dealer,* Nov. 14, 1971. With permission.

over sufficient time and in enough places to constitute a valid test, and by *small and direct,* I mean units of a size and structure that allow any individual citizen to feel that his voice is important in the decision-making processes of his community.

The argument will be offered that my assertion is "impractical" or "unrealistic." Almost no serious proposal is impractical until it is tried. Abandoning the use of leeches as medical accomplices was considered impractical, even radical by some, but one suspects that the practicality test is often used to establish who will have to change or yield or both. Whether or not I am realistic may depend upon which sets of data one consults and how the data is interpreted. For example, not all inequality of education is the sole product of racism, as some militant blacks claim.

> All the research of the last four decades points to the conclusion that differences in nutrition, general health, and access to intellectual and cognitive stimulation—which, of course, vary widely by social and economic status, and therefore by race, are the chief environmental determinants of children's intellectual performance. Eliminating racial distortions would improve ghetto education, but it would probably not eliminate disparities in achievement that are ultimately due to differences in social class.[11]

It is true that white America seems to be moving very slowly toward integration in housing. Racism still prevails in all too many situations, even though the 1970 census does indicate significant movement of blacks into suburbia and, indeed, of the poor into suburbia or its fringes. The census data indicates that 21 percent of the poor now live in the metropolitan areas around the central cities. But the trend toward dispersion of the poor is not the real issue. There is no conclusive evidence that irrevocably links education and housing. The neighborhood school is as much fiction as it is fact,

[11]David K. Cohen, op. cit., p. 27. With permission.

and where it has been abandoned as a guiding organizational concept, there is little evidence that any disaster has resulted. When Berkeley, California, integrated its schools, totally, it did so by the simple device of ruling that if you wanted primary education, you went to schools in one part of town, and if you wanted intermediate education, you went to school in another. Junior high schools were by grade, not service area. The result is that everyone will be bused at one time or another in his school career. It is significant that all of the people had the opportunity to vote for such a plan (a majority favored it), and all of the people continued to have the opportunity in subsequent votes (and a majority continues to support the plan). Blacks, Chicanos, and Orientals, who make up the minority population of Berkeley, are equally represented in all schools. In addition, participation in school community activities such as PTA now requires that parents travel out of their own neighborhoods, but that too has been accepted. In spite of this, there is no evidence that Berkeley is solely inhabited either by eccentrics or fools.

It is not possible to leave the discussion of Berkeley without commenting on the controversy surrounding its Black House and Casa de la Raza. Berkeley school authorities who had dealt honestly and openly with interracial strife and group aspirations recognized that there would be some black students and some Chicano students who, because of the long and most often frustrating struggle for equality and identity, would still be too angry to cope with the totally integrated setting. Black House and Casa de la Raza offered an alternate to these students, a way station on the path to some new and as yet undefined accommodation or reconciliation between the militant minority and the majority society. They were optional self-segregation devices; students could choose one of these alternatives, yet retain the right to reenter the regular schools when they wished.

Investigators from one senator's office were quick to call the arrangement "resegregation," which would have been true if the school district had been forcing students into Black House and Casa de la Raza. Segregation requires that someone is forcing someone else against his will to remain apart. This was not the case in Berkeley. It may be anticipated that clever lawyers, probably representing segregationist interests, will leap upon the Berkeley experiment and attempt to twist fact and intention either to achieve resegregation in their own states or destroy the legitimacy of Berkeley's plan.

David K. Cohen is less hopeful than I am about the general outlook.

> Is there a way out of our present morass? . . . One might still imagine that a massive assault on status disparities would shift attention away from the question of legitimacy, but it is hard to conceive of such an assault being mounted. Producing the needed legislation would require sustained political mobilization of blacks and whites, a prospect which seems remote so long as: a) they are so fatally preoccupied with each other; b) new money cannot be found to reduce the competition and allow recruitment of a broader constituency; and c) many powerful whites and ambitious blacks, for their separate reasons, prefer a political settlement to economic and social justice.[12]

White resistance in the matter of housing is not duplicated either in degree or kind in economics, politics, or education, once one divorces it from housing. Demographic data in both the 1960 and 1970 censuses indicate that minority groups have made sharp gains in many areas. The problem may be that these gains fall short of expectations or it may be that they occur so gradually that neither blacks nor whites recognize any dramatic change. When many things are changing rapidly in one's environment, it is easy to assume that change is a constant and difficult to notice each

[12]David K. Cohen, op. cit., p. 30. With permission. See also Thomas R. Dye and Brett W. Hawkins (eds.), *Politics in the Metropolis,* Merrill, Columbus, Ohio, 1967, for discussions on conflict management in cities.

instance of it. Social change always seems slower than necessary to those who advocate it, and much too fast for those who resist it. Social change usually has an even slower pace in a democracy since people have to battle out their cleavages and try to achieve consensus.

> Democracy is a social mechanism for resolving the problems of societal decision-making among conflicting interest groups with minimal force and maximum consensus. A stable democratic system requires sources of cleavage so that there will be struggle over ruling positions, challenges to parties in power, and shifts of parties in office; but without consensus—a value system allowing the peaceful "play" of power, the adherence by the "outs" to decisions made by "ins" and the recognition by "ins" of the rights of "outs"—there can be no democracy.[13]

Community participation in the schools is a significant way for citizens to regain a lost sense of community. It could supply each of us with a common cultural attitude or purpose, a sense of being a part of an ongoing process, a membership in a potentially dynamic social institution, and an identity, a status in life, if you will. The alternatives to this achievement may not be as satisfying to behold. For example, the alternative to a sense of community may be a form of authoritarianism. It is easy to concede Nisbet's[14] point that the decline of the primary institutions in life, i.e., the family, the church, and the neighborhood, demands that they in some way be replaced. It is by no means certain, however, that an authoritarian state need be the only substitute, although one must recognize that

[13]Seymour M. Lipset, "Political Sociology," in Robert K. Merton, Leonard Brown, and Leonard S. Cottrell, Jr. (eds.), *Sociology Today,* Basic Books, New York, 1959, p. 92. With permission. See also Calvin J. Larson and Philo C. Washburn (eds.), *Power, Participation and Ideology,* McKay, New York, 1969, for useful discussions of the interplay of political forces in a democracy.
[14]Robert A. Nisbet, *The Quest for Community,* Oxford, New York, 1953.

authoritarianism is one possible alternative. Other reasonable possibilities are a strong, organized interest group (perhaps ethnic in origin), a reconstituted local community, and even a functioning democracy. Mumford sees education as the central focus of city life, providing, of course, that it is committed to the goal of personal development, not social conformity.

> Participation in any constructive enterprise is, in itself, not without considerable value for the participant. It fulfills the human need for contact with fellow men. It relieves the isolation to which, in some degree, everyone is subject and which, carried to the extreme, grows into alienation. Participation tends to enhance self-esteem; the very act of involvement with others is some proof to the participant that he is accepted and that, even if his role is minor, he is not without worth. Participation is also likely to provide the individual with some intellectual stimulus through his exposure to the viewpoints of others. If only because it is a form of experience, participation is educational in the broadest sense. In interpersonal terms, it teaches—at least at the subconscious level—the dynamics of "give and take," of power relationships, and of planning and working toward goals.[15]

This participation must, of course, be real, not fanciful, hypothetical, or symbolic. Authentic participation may threaten the educational professional's self-concept, which has always been tinged with illusions of medical or legal autonomy and prestige. These professionals will find it strenuous to deal with the democratic processes. After all, most educators have been trained in the didactic school, despite Laura Zirbes's admonition that "if you want to be a teller, go to work in a bank." Dentler's criticisms of educational programs proposed by community-action programs (CAP) boil down to their evident lack of any real innovation and the

[15]Mario Fantini, Marilyn Gittell, and Richard Magat, *Community Control and the Urban School,* Praeger, New York, 1960, p. 173. With permission.

fact that none bear the "earmarks of citizen participation."[16] My own experience reviewing CAP proposals confirms Dentler's appraisal. The reason usually turned out to be that the school district had either captured control of the CAP agency or had at least negotiated an accommodation with the person in power. Many school districts, like municipalities, saw in community-action programs a chance to intercept additional funds from the federal government at the same time that they garnered a ready-made reputation for community involvement. Although poverty communities were for the most part powerless to prevent this harvesting of funds that had been intended for more substantial changes, they were usually aware of the plundering, and it only added to their growing disillusionment.

Daniel Moynihan provides the following quotation from Aaron Wildarsky facing the title page of his autobiographical analysis of community-action programs.

> A recipe for violence: Promise a lot; deliver a little. Lead people to believe they will be much better off, but let there be no dramatic improvement. Try a variety of small programs, each interesting but marginal in impact and severely under financed. Avoid any attempted solution remotely comparable in size to the dimensions of the problem you are trying to solve. Have middle class civil servants hire upper class student radicals to use lower class Negroes as a battering ram against the existing local political systems; then complain that people are going around disrupting things and chastise local politicians for not cooperating with those out to do them in. Get some poor people involved in local decision-making, only to discover that there is not enough at stake to be worth bothering about. Feel guilty about what has happened to black people; tell them you are surprised they have not revolted before; express shock and

[16]Robert A. Dentler, "A Critique of Education Projects in Community Action Programs," in Robert A. Dentler, Bernard Mackler, and Mary Ellen Warshaner (eds.), *The Urban R's,* Praeger (published for the Center for Urban Education), New York, 1967, pp. 158–162.

dismay when they follow your advice. Go in for a little force, just enough to anger, not enough to discourage. Feel guilty again; say you are surprised that worse has not happened. Alternate with a little suppression. Mix well, apply a match, and run. . . .[17]

Many antipoverty programs with grandiose educational components died precisely because Wildarsky's formula was followed almost to the letter. The ultimate irony came when the demise of such programs and tactics was blamed on poor people and used to prove that they could not be trusted to run their own affairs. My own observation is that poor people rarely got the chance, and if they did and made even the slightest mistake in the process, they were then pilloried as incompetent and untrustworthy.

Rempson's review of the historical roots of home-school relations[18] reveals that schools traditionally turn to the community only when they need money. Poverty communities are not usually considered to be rich lodes of financial support, but they do have considerable potential voting power; their votes can in many cities, and the number is growing steadily, make or break a tax levy or a bond issue. In short, they do have leverage, but they are often manipulated. If they vote against a tax levy or bond issue and do so without public explanation (the poor rarely have access to the mass media to explain their votes), it is construed by school authorities as "a vote against children." This charge is misleading and intimidating, and the poor are often cowed by it into giving blanket support to the schools that they know are committing what they call "intellectual genocide" on their children. Conversely, a vote for a tax levy or bond issue is ground for an immediate claim by the board or the superintendent that their superb efforts in behalf of poor children are heartily endorsed. It is difficult for the poor to obtain educational

[17]Daniel P. Moynihan, *Maximum Feasible Misunderstanding,* Free Press, New York, 1970, p. ii. With permission.
[18]Joe L. Rempson, "School-Parent Programs in Depressed Urban Neighborhoods," in Dentler et al., op. cit., p. 130.

change under these rules. We also know that "persons of low socio-economic status participate in indigenous and relatively informal groups," but much less "in formal voluntary organizations than do persons of higher socioeconomic status." This may be "because they: lack contact with people who do participate in such organizations; lack the ability to communicate in group situations; have no cultural expectations that would lead them to participate; do not see the relevance of participation to their needs; and lack the time and energy required for participation."[19]

There are, however, solutions to the problem. Rempson goes on to develop a very useful set of guidelines, each based upon multiple research findings, which should enable the sincere educator to develop a program of legitimate parent participation. The guidelines feature such things as commitment of full-time personnel, either lay or professional, to the effort; recognition that oral communication is better than written (for personal relationships and because it is the most common mode of communication); stress on social interaction; and the need that the program meet the "total educational, cultural, recreational, social and economic needs of the children, youth and adults of the neighborhood."[20]

What I have been saying thus far adds up to the simple question: Who owns the power in American society? It is clear that, at present, very little power is owned by the poor, or minority groups, or, for that matter, the average man. Whatever one sees as the pattern of concentration of power, from the late C. Wright Mills's version in his *Power Elite*[21] to any one of a number of conspiracy theories, the danger to democracy is clear and present. Redistribution of power, its dispersion to a wider and more democratic base, has become an urgent matter in the light of the increasing polarizations and conflicts that can rend and tear the fabric of our future. The dysfunctionalism of institutionized education is but a symptom of a wider malaise, the

[19]Rempson, op. cit., p. 135. With permission.
[20]Rempson, op. cit., pp. 138–141. With permission.
[21]C. Wright Mills, *The Power Elite,* Oxford, New York, 1957.

systematic erosion of the common man's power to control his own options.

It was at least the intent of the early poverty-war strategists to begin a process of renewal, a renovation of the seemingly lost arts of democratic living. The effort was to be focused upon those groups that economic, political, and social events had moved the farthest from both the processes and products of democracy. The strategies suggested were applicable in any community. They could be utilized to attack problems in housing, employment, the administration of justice, health, and a host of other arenas, including education. They invited what William W. Biddle called "the rediscovery of local initiative."[22]

The specific techniques to be used to organize and unleash "people power" to face common problems and work cooperatively on solutions became known as the *community-development process.* This term is not to be confused with things like chamber of commerce urban-renewal programs. Social improvement (and, it is hoped, educational improvement) is the general goal, but it is the process itself that is important as it attempts to restore faith in a democratic people so that they can indeed live, grow, and control their own destinies.

> Improvement is evaluated in terms of democratic skills, responsibility to serve a growing awareness of a common good, ethical sensitivity, and willingness to cooperate. All other improvements are judged good or bad by reference to what is happening to the people involved. Most articulate authorities in the field are coming to accept such criteria. Most will accept also that such favorable development in persons is brought about, not so much by what is done to benefit these persons, as by the decisions for action that they make for themselves.[23]

[22]William W. Biddle with Loureide J. Biddle, *The Community Development Process,* Holt, New York, 1965. Copyright © 1965 by Holt, Rinehart and Winston, Inc. Reprinted by permission of Holt, Rinehart and Winston, Inc.
[23]Ibid., p. 3. With permission.

The application of the community-development process to education promises both substantive and sociopsychological gains. These rewards are worth pursuing, although jaundiced educators may wonder what possible good can come from it. Community people, after all, are not professionally trained to solve complex educational problems. They are, however, capable of reliably reporting the impact of the educational process, and, as experts in providing feedback—the missing part of most educational evaluations and assessments—they have insights and solutions usually unknown or overlooked by the didactic school.

Consider the following exchange reported to me in Watts.

school counselor Mrs._____, your son just doesn't know how to read.

community mother I know. That is why I sent him to school.

Here the community person clearly delineates the responsibility of the school. She acknowledges its expertise and insists that it accept its responsibility, not push its failure back upon her. The problem of teaching a child to read is not a community problem, it is a school problem. Community involvement does not shift anyone's role. When a black high school girl says, again in Watts, "What's the good of all this education if I just end up working in somebody's kitchen?" she has raised an issue that both the school and the community can work cooperatively to solve. Or, let us say, a teacher has raised a question about why so few of her Chicano parents come to school for open house or parent conferences. Here again is a problem that the school cannot and should not try to solve alone, anymore than it should confront the problems of ethnic studies without reference to the ethnic community.

Biddle suggests that community development must begin with a primary group of people working in face-to-face relationship with one another, who can discover the participation process, organize it, and make it work.[24] It would be a voluntary association, associated with an individual school, informal at first, probably indigenous, and would usually contain some people who already are friends, who are concerned about school problems, and who are not yet so embittered that working with school people is impossible. The group should also contain a worker, sometimes called "an encourager," sometimes "a developer," who is highly trained in the skills of such an operation. Biddle calls such a group a "nucleus" and proposes the following outline for the flow of the process,[25] adapted here to fit the educational setting.

major stages	detailed events
EXPLORATORY	History—preliminary study for the developer
	Present events—information to guide the developer
	Invitation—should come to developer from some community person but could be school originated
	Introduction—of the developer to the group
	Informal conversations—the responsibility of the developer to initiate

It is important in the exploratory phase that educators understand that many urban poor people prize personal contact as an absolutely necessary first step. They want to know who you are, where you are "at," and to sense you as a person before plunging into business.

ORGANIZATIONAL	Problem—of obvious interest and concern to the community people
	Informal meetings—of the interested citizens

[24]Ibid., pp. 88–89.
[25]Ibid., pp. 90–91. With permission.

Structure—set up by the people who are to work on the problem

Commitment—by the citizens to continue working on such problems

Discussional training—using outside resources as often as necessary

DISCUSSIONAL   Definitions—of the problem, setting limits for discussion

Alternatives—varieties of solutions to the problem

Study—of the advantages and disadvantages of the proposed solutions

Value basis—principles to guide the evaluation of alternatives (for example, the educational commitments of the multicultural education listed in Chapter Three)

Decision—selection of a proposed action to solve the problem

ACTION   Work project—that carries the decision into action

Reporting—on the work done and on its effectiveness

Analysis—in discussions

Evaluation—critical judgment upon the work done

NEW PROJECTS   Repeat—discussion and action on new or redefined problems

Outside contacts—with the agencies and the people of power in the larger community

Increase of controversy—new problems increase in size and amount of conflict involved

Pressure action—controversy may call for pressure upon the "powers that be"

Need for coalition—contacts with outside powers call for working with other nucleus groups

CONTINUATION
Permanent nucleus—commitment changes to indefinite continuation of the nucleus

Withdrawal—by the community developer

Problems of increasing complexity—undertaken by the nucleus

Increasing responsibility—to deal with more complex problems

Proliferation—the splintering or colonizing of new nucleus groups to broaden participation

The aims of the program of community participation are, of course, the growth of the participants and the solution of educational problems in which the community is involved. The program should therefore reflect the concerns of the community people and not be imposed by the school. The natural patterns of interaction among the people will probably produce greater results than any managed arrangements by the school. Obviously, school people cannot approach the problems that are developed in their traditional defensive stance, and when leadership emerges from the people, there should be no attempts to co-opt it. The real test of whether the school intends to promote or frustrate citizen growth and democracy will come when controversy arises. If, for example, the community settles on accountability problems, the school must recognize that as correct and consistent with our laws, and school people will, it is hoped, contribute to the resolution of issues rather than, because of their defensive attitude, compound the problems.

The community worker, trained in part by educational sociologists, is a new specialist in education. He should generally be described as follows:

(1)   He is trained to work with people on a cooperative, participative, non-authoritative basis. He should be able to work with widely different varieties of individuals and groups.

(2)   He should start where people are, to respect the rights of self-determination (within the general framework of community and society), and to serve as an enabler and resource.

(3)   He is accustomed to using a problem-solving approach, with its successive "steps": Recognition of need, analysis, planning, action, and evaluation.

(4)   He should have a good working knowledge of types of community resources, governmental and voluntary, and of community power structure.

(5)   His equipment normally includes skills important for community development. Among these are: (a) fact-finding, surveys and studies; (b) planning and program development; (c) conference, group process and committee operation; (d) organization and administration; (e) communication, verbal and written, education, interpretation, public relations, participation in meetings of various sorts; (f) negotiational and social action.

(6)   He is in liaison with other agencies and organizations.

(7)   He is frequently a specialist in community organization and a generalist on other areas.

(8)   He provides leadership in gathering the facts regarding community life.

(9)   He provides leadership in the diagnosis and interpretation of the findings and relates these to selected areas of sensitivity.

(10)   His function is to help people see crisis and he must be capable of responsible leadership in bringing to the attention of citizens the facts and ways and means of articulating their views.

(11)   He is capable of seeing when he should withdraw from his leadership role and allow indigenous leadership to assert itself.

(12)   He is knowledgeable and skillful enough in group processes to be able to help the citizens establish attainable goals and methods in reaching these objectives[26]

It is also a goal of the community participation program that educators grow in skill and knowledge and that this growth be applied to the educational field. It is necessary therefore that the school engage in research on and evaluation of the problems and processes in which it is engaged with the community. The educational sociologist can be a key figure in the development of this research. The diagram on the following page shows Biddle's design for the research process added to his scheme of the flow of action.[27]

It is entirely possible that the success of the individual school nucleus groups may lead to a total district plan of participation. Whether this needs to be a formal organization is debatable. If the focus of action is on problem-solving and participation, a formal districtwide organization of citizens might fall prey to politicians who see in such an organization any number of private advantages. One way school districts prevent community participation is to get the community involved in endless legalistic debates on every fine point of organizing a formal body. I know one urban district that applauds itself for the hours and hours of meetings it has held on creating a community participation mechanism, but after almost three years of such games, there is still no working organization and no community

[26]*Community Development in California,* symposium report of a conference at Asilomar, Calif., July 9–12, 1963, p. 19.
[27]Biddle, op. cit., p. 132. With permission.

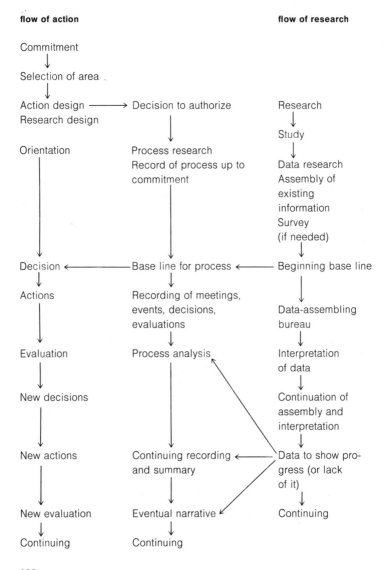

flow of action

flow of research

Commitment
↓
Selection of area
↓
Action design ——→ Decision to authorize   Research
Research design   ↓
                        ↓   Study
Orientation   Process research   ↓
                     Record of process up to   Data research
                     commitment   Assembly of
                                                 existing
                                                 information
                                                 Survey
                                                 (if needed)
                                                 ↓
Decision ←———————— Base line for process ←———————— Beginning base line
↓
Actions   Recording of meetings,   ↓
                     events, decisions,   Data-assembling
                     evaluations   bureau
↓   ↓
Evaluation   Process analysis   Interpretation
                                                 of data
↓   ↓
New decisions   Continuation of
                                                 assembly and
                                                 interpretation
↓   ↓
New actions   Continuing recording ←———— Data to show pro-
                     and summary   gress (or lack
                                                 of it)
↓   ↓   ↓
New evaluation   Eventual narrative ←   Continuing
↓   ↓
Continuing   Continuing

participation. It is likely that in the future this district will have difficulty convincing the community people it is sincere about wanting genuine participation. In such cases, the community usually organizes against the schools instead of with them.

Community participation is not a piece of cake. There will be conflict and controversy, but then, as I said earlier, democracy involves both cleavage and consensus. The educational leader can call upon increasing resources to assist him in understanding this conflict.[28] The educational sociologist is one such resource in this area.

Critics of community participation sooner or later raise the issue of its relation to quality education. It is often their assertion that there is no evidence that community participation will raise the quality of education, but that there is ample reason to believe it will raise the blood pressure of already harried educators. It is not easy to answer this criticism. There is, for a fact, little evidence one way or the other because the kind of community participation I have outlined here has never been extensively tried, much less researched. For conservative educators, this is convenient. They feel that nothing should be tried until it has been proven conclusively somewhere else. This is reminiscent of the politician who claims, "I can't do anything unless I get elected, but I can't get elected if I do anything."

But the more basic question is: What is quality education? If by quality we mean achievement as measured by standardized tests designed within the limits of the single-product model, then it is difficult to see how community participation's impact will produce, one for one, increased point scores on these tests, at least at first. We have no way of knowing precisely how enhanced self-concepts of parents and other community people will affect

[28]James S. Coleman, *Community Conflict,* Free Press, New York, 1957. This monograph is a publication of the Bureau of Applied Social Research at Columbia University. It contains an excellent bibliography of research and comment on this issue.

children's achievement scores on any standardized measures. Similarly, we have no way of knowing what the impact will be if the school and the community become genuine partners instead of enemies.

If we define the effects of quality education as: (1) Increasing self-fulfillment; (2) growing democratic skills; and (3) proficiency in fundamental academic skills, tested with a broad range of measures devoid of any universal best standard, cultural or class bias, and without predefinition of what constitutes prestigious career choices, then we may, in fact, discover that community participation does promote quality education. Obviously some parts of our definition of quality are exempt from direct professional influence. Educators often are inclined to assume that quality is singularly related to the exercise of their professional functions. However, "the improvement of professional function without democratic process is technocracy,"[29] and that is not a goal we are seeking to promote in public education.

It is entirely possible that poverty and minority parents, if given the opportunity to choose, will insist upon a return to the most traditional kinds of education. If they perceive that traditional education has been a primary source of the advantage of rich over poor and white over black, then they may well seek that traditional education. I found this to be true in the middle 1960s in urban poverty communities in such diverse cities as Los Angeles, New Orleans, Detroit, Boston, Cleveland, and San Francisco. Any "new" education was viewed with suspicion; it might be just another trick. I suspect that this attitude is changing as poor and minority-group parents hear more and more middle-class parents publicly denouncing traditional education as being equally dysfunctional for their children. Particularly in the urban community, the definition of quality may be undergoing change.

Professional educators who criticize community participation usually do so because community participation appears to

[29]Mario Fantini, Marilyn Gittell, and Richard Magat, *Community Control and the Urban School,* Praeger, New York, 1960, p. 175.

them to be a threat to their professionalism. It bears repeating that this is a technocratic consideration and not appropriate to public education in a *democracy*. It must also be remembered that the school as a social system does not stand in splendid isolation; "it interlocks with other social systems—political, economic, familial— and its structure and function cannot be fully understood without reference to the other systems."[30] The insistence upon professional chastity is out of place.

More fundamentally, urban community people have a right to raise serious questions about the professionalism of the current educational establishment when they view the dysfunctionalism of the education provided their children. If a doctor lost as many patients as urban schools lose students, or if a lawyer failed as many clients as urban educators have failed their clients, there would be serious question about their professionalism too. In other words, professionalism is an achieved status, as opposed to an ascribed status. This means that the educator must earn his status, and he must continuously perform well enough to retain it. Perhaps the emerging definition of a professional will be that he is one who is able to change his procedures in the light of new evidence. Community participation is a rich source of such data.

[30]Herbert A. Thelen and Jacob W. Getzels, "The Social Sciences: Conceptual Framework for Education," *School Review,* vol. 65, no. 8, pp. 351–352, Autumn 1957.

chapter six

youth:
the demand
for alternatives

Surely one of the most perplexing developments in American education and social life has been the emergence of a distinct youth culture. It is a confusing "movement" because it is so difficult to pin down, classify, and dissect, but it is real. One has the sense of being surrounded by it, yet at times it is as amorphous as a drifting fog, as solid as a brick thrown at a cop, or as tender as a couple making love in a public park. It is, at once, change, response, a new vision, a self-indulgence, a wry challenge, and a bloody revolt. It is felt in all levels of schooling and materializes in every social institution, touching all styles of life, customs, and mores. All the indicators seem to agree that, in one form or another, it is here to stay.

The first nationally recognized manifestation of a student revolt happened at the University of California at Berkeley in the fall of 1964. It was spawned in the students' idealistic activism in the civil-rights movement, and strangely, came into being as the result of a parochial struggle between the forces of Governor William Scranton and Senator Barry Goldwater during the Republican National Convention of 1964, held across the bay in San Francisco. The precipitating issue was whether Scranton supporters could recruit convention demonstrators from the University of California campus. Goldwater supporters, led by University Regent William F. Knowland, tried to prevent it. The slogan that emerged from the students' uprising against such restrictions was "Free speech"; later, as the struggle widened, students chanted "Make love, not war," "Power to the people," and a host of other equally undefined slogans that allowed wide individual interpretation and, therefore, wide individual behavioral response. The slogan that ultimately nominated Senator Goldwater at the 1964 Republican Convention was "In your heart you know he's right," which is as undefined as the students' slogans and as susceptible to a wide range of uses. Both groups claimed to be striking out for individual freedom and the achievement of an impossible but highly desirable dream. Both saw their movements as great moral causes and the self-evident salvation of American civilization.

Yet a strange precision, a sharpness of vision, marked this split between generations and philosophies. Using Margaret Mead's typology,[1] the Republicans were appealing for a return to a *post-figurative* culture where what went before (ideals, values, customs, etc.) became the model for the present and, indeed, the

[1]Margaret Mead, *Culture and Commitment,* Natural History Press (Doubleday), Garden City, N.Y., 1970.

future. It was essentially a nineteenth-century model of maximum free competition. This was what its adherents believed had brought America to the pinnacle of world economic and political strength. The youth, on the other hand, were calling for a *pre-figurative* culture, a culture where change comes so quickly that neither the past nor the present can be relevant models for the future. Caught in between was the *co-figurative* culture where the past is conceived as only partially useful, the present needs constant adjustment, and the future looms ahead as a great and sometimes dreaded unknown. As this conflict of cultures grew, it was clear that the Establishment proponents of post-figurative and co-figurative cultures held the heights, but it was also clear that youth would not fight conventional battles. Their "revolution" was to be different and that is precisely why it has been so disconcerting. It has not been conducted by Roberts' Rules of Order, or the Marquis of Queensberry Rules, or Hoyle, or any other known and established system. It is, in fact, antisystem, antiorder, a topsy-turvy movement that is at once erratic, charming, violent, gentle, maddening, and beautiful. It raises penetrating and impertinent questions and then walks away without waiting for an answer. It embraces the unconventional conventionally and scorns the conventional unconventionally. In short, it challenges most definitions based upon past premises or present customs. It challenges the way we were educated and the ways in which we think about problems, and it even questions if we know what the real problems are.

Charles A. Reich, in *The Greening of America,* gives as good a list as anyone of the perceptions of the counterculture, what they think is wrong with America, and why they insist that the times are changing.

1   Disorder, corruption, hypocrisy, war.

2   Poverty, distorted priorities, and law-making by private power.

3   Uncontrolled technology and the destruction of environment.

4   Decline of democracy and liberty; powerlessness.

5   The artificiality of work and culture.

6   Absence of community.

7   Loss of self.[2]

Point by point, the "Fair Witness"[3] would have to admit that there is considerable validity to the charges. There is little to argue but degree. It is the solutions that youth proposes that stir controversy. For example, the argument offered by national adult leaders, all the way up to the President, is that young people should "work within the system." Youth leaders were quick to recognize the trap involved. Obviously the system was organized so that those currently holding superior power would continue to exercise their control. They made the rules and enforced them. To work within the system's rules simply meant maintenance of the present power allocations and no significant change. Direct and violent confrontation with the system was also no alternative because the system was too physically powerful (police, troops, etc.)to be challenged in that manner. Besides, much of the youth culture was basically oriented toward nonviolence as a result of the influence of Martin Luther King, the words of Thoreau and Gandhi, and the inherent gentleness in the movement.

"Working within the system" came to have a new definition. It meant being there, but not cooperating. It meant participating, but on one's own terms, independent and unintimidated by threats of

[2]Charles A. Reich, *The Greening of America,* Random House, New York, 1970. Citations are from the Bantam edition, pp. 4–7.
[3]See Robert Heinlein, *Strangers in a Strange Land,* Berkley Medallion Books, New York, 1968 (a well-read book among young people).

"conform or we'll cut you out," since the scene from which one would be exiled was economic rather than personal, and economic values were not worshipped.

Reich uses the classifications Consciousness I to roughly represent the post-figurative culture and Consciousness II to indicate the co-figurative culture. He asserts that both have failed since neither is appropriate to the world in which we now live. The counterculture, or Consciousness III (the pre-figurative), even considers Consciousness I and II to be destructive to the survival of a free and open America, and certainly not cultures into which they wish to be inducted.

Consciousness III rejects "competition, rivalry, or personal flights of ego and power" as "socially destructive."[4] It seeks "to replace the infantile and destructive self-seeking that we laud as competition by a new capacity for working and living together."[5]

> The view of human nature we have held to so long is based on materialism. It is not "man" we knew, but "economic man." "Self-interest" was defined in material terms. It is "economic man" who is aggressive, competitive, eager to win in sports or in life, eager for status and power, jealous and envious, unwilling to share his private property, intensely privatistic about his family, relating to all others primarily in ways defined by his interests.[6]

In contrast, Consciousness III proposes:

> . . . a community devoted to the search for wisdom, [when] the true relationship between people is that all are students and all are teachers. Teaching in this sense consists of helping each person with his own personal search for experience and his own goals. Although the goals are individual, it is apparent that the

[4]Reich, op. cit., p. 384. With permission.
[5]Ibid., p. 387. With permission.
[6]Ibid., p. 416. With permission.

search for self cannot take place in isolation, that self must be realized in a community, and therefore the community enhances each person no matter what his particular endeavor.[7]

"The new generation insists upon being open to all experience . . ."[8] and finds joy and a better, even higher, reason in such pursuits. It refuses to be cast in a mold, either of someone else's choosing or its own. It insists on "staying loose," prepared to move in any direction down any road where deeper personal meaning might be found. It wants technology to be its slave, not the reverse; it finds the power of the future in people, not machines. Consciousness III abhors the exploitation of men by other men but insists that every man exploit himself, in the sense that he turn every experience into both practical and aesthetic use.

This new consciousness, called the counterculture, will, Reich claims, revolutionize the structure of society. "It does not accomplish this by direct political means, but by changing culture and the quality of individual lives, which in turn changes politics and, ultimately, structure."[9] It believes that "there are no enemies. There are no people who would not be better off, none who do not, in the depth of their beings, want what Consciousness III wants."[10]

A somewhat distorted interpretation of the counterculture, built as it is on what Kenneth Lash calls "the children of turmoil,"[11] is the idea that young people simply are crying out for what they call relevance. Culbert and Elden, trying to reassure the businessman, state:

> . . . he is articulating a desire to take responsibility, to make decisions, and to learn from experience. In expecting a

[7]Ibid., p. 417. With permission.
[8]Ibid., p. 393. With permission.
[9]Ibid., p. 18.
[10]Ibid., pp. 428–429.
[11]Kenneth Lash, "Children of Turmoil," *Change,* vol. 3, no. 2, pp. 8–9, March-April 1971.

corporation to become relevant, young people are expecting it to take responsibility, to make decisions, and to learn from experience, especially in the case of social matters. They believe an organization, to have a right to exist, must be willing to ask what it can do in relation to what ought to be done.

The answer to this question, they feel, must come both from within and from outside the corporation: (a) from management, (b) from those other corporate members who have had little opportunity in the past to help choose company directions and policies, (c) from company clientele, and (d) from those outside the company who are deeply concerned with what direction the company shall pursue.[12]

Corporate responsibility, however, is really not the thrust of the counterculture's program. Admittedly, it is not always clear what is. The problem in trying to deal with youth today lies in knowing whether their reactions are rational, or neurotic, or facetious. Like very young children, older youth are blessed with flashes of genuinely profound insight with an accompanying intense commitment. But it is often haphazard, for they are also capable of pronouncements of incredibly naive tomfoolery. Part of their charm is in their intensity of feeling, their evident sincerity, and often the blazing purity of their spirit. Although it may be chic in some quarters to hang upon their every word and deed, young people, like any other group, should never be considered, ipso facto, wise, factual, or even logical. That is, their affective insights may not be equal to their cognitive insights. The solution for adults may be to have the courage and skill to identify clearly the hokum without hurting, or "putting down," the young persons who proclaim it. This demands wisdom, patience, love, and understanding of this most exciting, erratic, vulnerable, but determined group. For all their problems,

[12]Samuel A. Culbert and James M. Elden, "An Anatomy of Activism for Executives," *Harvard Business Review,* vol. 48, no. 6, pp. 141–142, November-December 1970. With permission.

they may ultimately be right, even though occasionally it might be for the wrong reasons.

Certainly youth's profound aversion to the blatant hypocrisies in our society cannot be criticized. For example, young people rightfully point to the many kinds of authoritarianism practiced daily in our democracy. Indeed, Americans have learned to be subjects to authority. Youth, on the other hand, has learned the ideals of a free democracy, but finds that those ideals are honored only when they do not seem to challenge established authority. They are impatient with the rationalization that since democratic procedures established the authority, it is legitimate. What they have not yet confronted may be the idea that most Americans, although taught the ideals of democracy in school, rarely have much opportunity to practice then. Most Americans do not work for a living in democratic organizations; they are constantly subject to nondemocratic management and are soon conditioned to accept such authority or perish economically and socially. Young people who have yet to face this conditioning are, for the moment, intelligent enough to perceive the dilemma and even act upon it without fear of reprisal.

If Shelley were alive today, or Blake, or Keats, or any one of a dozen romantic English poets, he would surely be a part of the counterculture. He would be at every folk-rock concert, leading campus revolts, campaigning against the war in Vietnam, or be much involved in the campaigns of candidates of the left, or perhaps even the far right, where romanticism also thrives. Was Shelley "on a trip" when he fell out of his boat and stayed on the bottom because it was so beautiful down there? Was Byron in Greece or was he with Che? Did De Quincy get his "dope" in Haight-Ashbury? Was Wordsworth on a hitchhiking trip when he spied the yellow daffodils? Perhaps not, but surely such men would be at home with J. R. R. Tolkien's latest fantasy; they would be comfortable with the affective imagery of the social and political slogans of the counterculture and with its ofttimes Peter Pan philosophies.

Professor Philip Gleason documents the case of the new

romanticism and says: "Whatever it may have been in essence, romanticism developed in a revolutionary period and was both part of and a reaction to a profound upheaval in Western civilization."[13] Certainly conditions today are remarkably similar and youth may feel that this time they will produce not only poetry but also social change. At least that is what any card-carrying romantic must feel, and that is what sustains him in his quest. What is this new world?

J. Anthony Lukas quotes a young radical who wants:

> An end to men's afflictions, an end to exploitation and oppression, an end to competitive and abusive social relationships, an end to the alienation between man and man, between man and woman, between men and nature, between intellectual and physical and artistic labor, between men's activity and their human selves; the beginning of men's collective mastery over their fate, of brotherhood as the functional principle of social relations, of material and cultural abundance for all, of the full development of each as the condition for the full development of all.[14]

Such goals do not seem radical enough to cause reasonable men to shudder. However, if they were stated in reverse, they would frighten even the most cynical among us.

Gleason refers to Ludwig Kahn's discussion of *Social Ideals in German Literature,* which, it is claimed, influenced the young Karl Marx.

> The romanticist, Kahn points out in the first paragraph of this chapter, looks to an association of free individuals joined together in perfect union. . . . Modifying the sociological classification introduced by Ferdinand Tonnies, says Kahn, we may

[13]Philip Gleason, "Our New Age of Romanticism," *America,* Oct. 7, 1967, p. 373. With permission.
[14]J. Anthony Lukas, *Don't Shoot—We Are Your Children!,* Random House, New York, 1971, p. 59. With permission.

> perhaps use the term community to denote this romantic ideal,
> in contrast to the classical society. This sort of community
> involves no external restraint on its individual members; rather,
> the community depends on individually differentiated men just
> as the organism depends on its discreet and specialized
> organs. . . . The romantics look forward to another golden age,
> a revival of a happy human community in which love and good
> will, not duty and principles, are the controlling forces.[15]

One might also turn to the trancendentalism of our own country, examining Emerson, Thoreau, Channing, and perhaps Bronson Alcott, the Peabody sisters, and Horace Mann. Was it their idealism, romantic as it may have been, that set a tone for the founding of American democracy? Lukas finds the continuity of generations in his examinations of the radical young of today.[16]

Indeed, his interpretation suggests not a counterculture, but a "consecutive culture." The new culture is clearly to be built upon romantic ideals proclaimed before, beginning far back in our American-European heritage. The consecutive culture then is not pre-figurative as such, but its romanticism makes it sound that way. Neither is it post-figurative, as the far right would wish, for their romanticism is not truly romantic, merely nostalgic. Consciousness III has, perhaps, always been the hope to which Con II or the co-figurative liberal has clung, since it makes the future something to look forward to rather than to fear.

Critics of the counterculture abound. But then, in their time, Shelley and Keats were not the favorites of the Establishment. No romantic is, because he deals so much at the affective level that he confounds the cognitive; and man as a thinking being does not easily yield his claim to rationality, as it is expressed in his elaborate cognitive modes. There are *angry* critics of the counterculture, particularly as expounded by Reich. Anger is an emotional re-

---

[15]Gleason, op. cit., p. 374. With permission.
[16]Lukas, op. cit., pp. 443–461.

sponse, and it is perhaps ironic that the defenders of cognitive analysis should become so affective in their objections. It may even suggest that other motives underlie their concern and opposition.[17]

One of the maddening things about the young people of the counterculture is that they are not impressed by the accomplishments of their elders. And that can be a threatening experience. After all, I worked hard in graduate school, got my doctorate, climbed up the academic ladder, and now someone should listen to me. It's only fair. And they should be impressed with what I have learned and can teach them. But they aren't. They are not even impressed by the critics who write in the *New Yorker*, or the *New York Times*, or the intellectual journals, and that is very disconcerting. To make matters worse, they do not even start an argument from any of the established premises that adults have so carefully nurtured and on which we depend to justify our own experience.

The easiest thing to do then is to cut them down, call them freaks and dope addicts and irresponsible know-nothings and do it cleverly in matchless prose that will add laurels to our already overcrowded brows. Let us call Reich, a Yale law professor, a traitor to his class or just another one of those radical, pink university people we pay to subvert our children. Perhaps we can admit, jealously, that Reich is on to something legitimate, but he is not as competent as we are to deal with it. Of course, there are those whose special commitments foreclose any interpretation of events that fails to agree with their own and those who must have a thorough discussion of the issues within the framework of their own specialties before they can relate.

Despite the critics and despite whatever weaknesses its spokesmen may reveal, the counterculture is real and apparently growing and, most importantly, it is already changing the nation and

[17]See Philip Nobile (ed.), *The Con III Controversy: The Critics Look at the Greening of America*, Pocket Books, New York, 1971.

perhaps the Western world. Pomposity, provincialism, and hurt egos may cause complaints, but this strange and exasperating movement is having impact. Because of this, it deserves the best of our attention.

The counterculture has been described by psychiatrist S. L. Halleck as follows:

1   Some students reject the political and economic status quo and are making vigorous attempts to change the structure of our society. These are the student activists.

2   Some students reject the values of their society as well as the values of their own past and are developing a style of life which is contradictory to the Western ethics of hard work, self-denial, success, and responsibility. These students sometimes participate in efforts to change the society, but for the most part they are withdrawn and passive. They can be described as alienated.

3   Both activist and alienated students tend to come from affluent middle- or upper-class homes. They are sensitive and perceptive individuals. They are also highly intelligent.

4   Both activist and alienated students have difficulty in relating to the adult generation. They are articulate, irreverent, humorless, and relentless in their contempt for what they view as adult hypocrisy. Such youth are highly peer-oriented. They turn to one another rather than their parents when shaping their belief systems or when seeking emotional support.

5   Alienated students and, to a lesser extent, activist students find it difficult to sustain goal-directed activity. Their capacity to organize for any kind of action is limited. They often fail at work or school. Even their political efforts seem highly disorganized.

6   Alienated students live at the edge of despair. Although they seem at times to be enjoying life, there is always a sense of

153

foreboding about them. Often they become depressed and suicidal. Activist students are more emotionally stable, but are also prone to deep feelings of hopelessness and self-pity.[18]

Two key points that Halleck does not make are: These youth are like the group from which we have, in the past, drawn our most dynamic leadership for the future; and they are also the group whom we have found are easily crushed by force or other tough responses, despite the fact that the use of such methods to over-whelm them, to bring them to line, usually only confirms for them *all* that they despise in the adult society. The tough response does not address itself to their central concern for consciousness. Whatever the details of its application, and critics will take issue with various details, the central point is still youth's emphasis upon conscious-ness, awareness, a new perspective, a fresh look that leads to a new logic, a new ordering of values and priorities. The tough response is to actions rather than ideas and, historically, has usually proven to be useful only for short-term repression, which only serves to strengthen the youth culture's convictions. If the young are radical, then repression only radicalizes them further. Radicalization only pushes youth to greater extensions of their alienation and despair.

One extension of alienation and despair that is disturb-ing is the new folkway of "ripping off" (stealing), even though it is a logical response to the rather constant and gigantic rip-offs of American business, accepted and carried out as a matter of course each working day. Youth will use a mirror response as they try again to call our attention to something we are doing that *we taught them was wrong.*

Much of the youth culture then is, in fact, consecutive; in many ways its values are the values that we adults instilled. Youth is often simply asking, and then demanding, that we live up to those

---

[18]S. L. Halleck, "Hypotheses of Student Unrest," *Phi Delta Kappan,* vol. 40, no. 1, p. 2, September 1968. With permission.

values. If we claim the Christian-Hebraic values, then we should live them. In our failure to do so, we only convince youth more and more that there must be a better way to achieve that ill-defined, amorphous, totally aware utopia they must find. The romantic tradition, after all, recognizes and even courts opposition and despair.

The youth consecutive culture is, of course, fraught with danger. Its excesses could be its undoing, as was the case with many an earlier romantic. Chatterton killed himself at seventeen. Shelley drowned at thirty; Keats was dead of consumption at twenty-six, Thomas De Quincey was a narcotic addict by thirty-six. Whatever is good and idealistic in the consecutive culture could be destroyed by drugs, taken first perhaps in the search for expansion of the mind and the new awareness, but also as an escape from a reality they cannot bear or do not wish to cope with in the usual ways. In the case of drugs, the dominance of the affective over the cognitive could be, and has been in too many cases, fatal, both to the individual and to the movement he wants so desperately to support.

Similarly, self-indulgence in the name of freedom can destroy, for freedom is not exploitation of others or irresponsibility to self, even in the lexicon of consecutive-culture values. Rejection by the "now generation" of everything but the spirit of the moment also has its costs and perils. Many of my students have yet to hear their own voices in the literature that preceded them.

They, themselves, are full of songs and poems of their own creation, often excellent, but at the same time, they are often totally void of remembrances of things past.

Have they read the *Preface to the 1855 Edition* of Walt Whitman's *Leaves of Grass?* Better still, do they know Whitman when he sings:

> *Listen! I will be honest with you,*
> *I do not offer the old smooth prizes, but offer rough new prizes,*
> *These are the days that must happen to you:*

You shall not keep up what is called riches,
You shall scatter with lavish hand all that you earn or achieve,
You but arrive at the city to which you were destined, you hardly
settle yourself to satisfaction before you are called by an
irresistive call to depart.
You shall be treated to the ironical smiles and mockings of
those who remain behind you,
What beckonings of love you receive you shall only answer with
passionate kisses of parting,
You shall not allow the hold of those who spread their reached
hands toward you.

From "Song of the Open Road," 1855

As I lay with my head in your lap camerado,
The confession I made I resume, what I said to you and the open
air I resume,
I know I am restless and make others so,
I know my words are weapons full of danger, full of death,
For I confront peace, security, and all the settled laws to unsettle
them,
I am more resolute because all have denied me that I could ever
have been had all accepted me.
I heed not and have never heeded either experience, cautions,
majorities, nor ridicule.
And the threat of what is called hell is little or nothing to me;
Dear camerado! I confess I have urged you onward with me,
and still urge you, without the least idea what is our
destination,
Or whether we shall be victorious, or utterly quelled and
defeated.

"As I Lay with My Head in Your Lap Camerado," 1855

The consecutive culture of youth emerged from what Max Lerner has called the "essence of the American revolutionary spirit" and in particular, from one outgrowth of that spirit, the

American educational system. At once, that emergence represents both the greatest strengths of the educational system and its greatest weaknesses. If we wish to know where the consecutive culture got its values, we can look to the schools. It is in the schools, not the family, that most youth learn the details of their culture, the form and structure and ideal functioning of the social, economic, and political institutions of the society. And many schools have done well their job of teaching the "ideal culture," the values and attitudes of ideal democracy, ideal humanitarianism, and ideal aesthetics. The remarkable thing is that so many schools have done so with such uncontested boredom, overpowering authoritarianism, and unquestionable hypocrisy.

The consecutive culture's first target for reform has been the schools: It was to schools that the first demands were made. Youths are in school; it is their milieu and their home ground. The issues in school are immediate; the youth communications systems are working at peak efficiency, and the anger with schooling is symbolic of all their other discontents. Student protests broke out on school grounds and campuses first; the Kent State students were killed *on campus,* as were the Jackson State students.

Gross, in summing up the principles of reform advocated by "radical" thinkers, both youthful and adult, develops the following list:

1   Students, not teachers, must be the center of education.

2   Teaching and learning should start and stay with the students' real concerns, rather than with artificial disciplines, bureaucratic requirements, or adults' rigid ideas about what children need to learn.

3   The paraphernalia of standard classroom practice should be abolished: Mechanical order, silence, tests, grades, lesson plans, hierarchial supervision and administration, homework, and compulsory attendance.

4   Most existing textbooks should be thrown out.

5   Schools should be much smaller and much more responsive to diverse educational needs of parents and children.

6   Certification requirements for teachers should be abolished.

7   All compulsory testing and grading, including intelligence testing and entrance examinations, should be abolished.

8   In all educational institutions supported by tax money or enjoying tax-exempt status, entrance examinations should be abolished.

9   Legal requirements which impede the formation of new schools by independent groups of parents—such as health and safety requirements—should be abolished.

10   The school monopoly on education should be broken. The best way to finance education might be to give every consumer a voucher for him to spend on his education as he chooses, instead of increasing allocations to the school authorities.[19]

It does not seem likely that these ten principles will soon be enacted. The American school system as a major social institution in our society, whatever its shortcomings, does succeed in serving the social, economical, and political interests of enough people, particularly powerful people, that it seems premature, and perhaps unrealistic, to predict any total victory for far-reaching reforms. But in their very statement and in the actions that have been taken thus far to implement them, we are receiving a message we cannot ignore.

[19]Ronald Gross, "From Innovations to Alternatives: A Decade of Change in Education," *Phi Delta Kappan,* vol. 53, no. 1, p. 23, September 1971. With permission.

The word *alternatives* is no longer radical. A host of free schools, schools without walls, commune learning centers, independent schools, and other alternatives to the faltering public school system have been springing up in every city and crossroads across the country. Often parents who claim to deplore the youth culture are organizing to present to that culture precisely what it is demanding. If that seems ironic, one need only recall that the post-World War II parent was determined to give his children "all the things he didn't have," mostly in the form of material ease and comfort. As a new generation of middle-class parents emerges, they too have dreams for their progeny, but material wealth for many is no longer a problem; material wealth is something they have. What they did not have, they feel, were good schools, and they will now set out to provide the kind of education "they didn't have."

The dysfunctionalism of urban schools that particularly hurts the poor and racial minority groups has not gone unnoticed. Education is still a key value in American society, so much so that white middle- and upper-class parents, striving for their own children, have also recognized that urban education must be reformed. While they may do very little directly about urban schools, most reform-minded parents in the suburbs will do little, consciously, to oppose urban educational reform per se. At least they remain passive until they are directly threatened, as in the case of integration. It is also clear that any reforms that penetrate the suburbs will be the models for reform in the cities. Suburban parents already enjoy a great deal of direct participation in their schools, and because of the smaller size of the suburban school districts, parents can and do hold their school officials more immediately accountable.

If the suburbs remain aloof and detached from the city, as in the present colonialist relationship, reform of the city will be extremely slow. On the other hand, if integration, tax equalization, or metropolitan government occur (and court decisions appear to be moving things in these directions), which inextricably link the fate of urban schools to suburban schools, then reform of urban schools will come with much greater rapidity. Colonial powers will not endure the dysfunctionalism of urban schools when it affects their children. The suburban colonial power structure can demand reforms and usually succeeds. The problem then will be what reforms are demanded. Here is where the middle- and upper-class-based leaders of the consecutive culture will have their greatest opportunity.

Many young people, as part of their commitment to the service of others, to the value of togetherness with all people, express a deep interest in social-service or related careers. Rejection of materialistic, commercial values plus the romanticism of helping the poor, the oppressed, and the underprivileged will lead some to consideration of educational careers. However, many of these same young people are increasingly rejecting the idea of joining the educational system as it is, in the standard roles it now offers, such as classroom-bound teaching. Instead they seek alternative careers, alternative schools, and alternative kinds of service. They are rapidly becoming the backbone of the alternative-schools movement, along with disenchanted young teachers who have tried the system and now reject it.

Many a college student who feels a thrust toward education almost categorically rejects the traditional roles in traditional schools. As students, they are antiauthoritarianism, antirigidity, anti-impersonality, and against the single-model–Dick and Jane competitive system they feel they would have to endure. Theirs is a revolt against structure as well as values. They want to design and implement new forms, and they are so convinced of the correctness and justice of their cause that they are unafraid of creating alternate schools that survive on a shoestring and are in direct competition with the better-financed and established public system.

The alternative schools they seek to create have one thing in common: Freedom of choice. Alternative education is perceived as being essentially the increasing of options for individuals in reality settings. The Parkway School in Philadelphia, even though it is operated by the system, is one alternative. It uses the city as its campus and the people of the city, with their many and varied occupations and perspectives, as its faculty. Similar schools exist elsewhere: Chicago has its Metro School, and in Cleveland, there is the independent Cleveland Urban Learning Community (CULC).

Father Tom Shea, the founder of CULC, states its philosophy when he says: "School is wherever it happens, since school is not a place, it is you." Shea states CULC's goals as:

1   Bring a group of high school age youth together from every part of the City of Cleveland and its suburbs to learn with and from each other.

2   Allow students to seek out, design, and document their own learning experiences.

3   Relate education to and through people who are using their knowledge in careers and various ways of life.

4   Maintain an open process of decision-making about courses and the government of the school.[20]

CULC is presently approved by the Department of Education of the State of Ohio and is sponsored by a parochial high school and various local philanthropic foundations.

The openness of the Adams High School in Portland, Oregon, is another example of the school system sponsoring its own alternative. The Urban League and its Street Academy program is an alternative outside the system, as are dozens of small, private, free or tuitional schools, all with some special new feature, that have popped up all across the country. Some were created to maintain an ethnic or religious identity. Some are housed in converted churches or factories (for example, the Newark "parent-powered" school) or

[20]Statement of the Cleveland Urban Learning Community, 1971. With permission.

even older homes, and each does its special pleading for options its sponsors do not feel are available through the public system. Many will not survive more than a year or two because they are faced with the continuing need for money from philanthropic sources. But if present indications are predictive, as one school fails, another two will spring up to take its place.

Colleges and universities that train people for positions in the public schools now have the challenge to train people for alternative schools. It seems obvious that higher education cannot be tied to public elementary and secondary schools in any exclusive service relationship. In fact, it may be that the most responsible thing a university can do is to provoke experimentation, either by direct influence on lower schools or by assisting in the creation of workable alternatives. For college students interested in careers in the alternative schools, training must be available. Here is one such program.[21]

ALTERNATIVE SCHOOL FORMS TRAINING SEQUENCE

sophomore year

1 *Assessment of current education*   3 credit hours
A survey of current educational purposes, patterns, practices, and the problems generated therein. The course perspective will be that of both the social sciences and the humanities rather than of traditional professional education. Frequent observation of current schooling will be required, since this course will constitute the base point from which to launch inquiry into alternatives.

2 *Alternative forms of education*   3 credit hours
A survey of literature presently available on all known alternative forms of education, including the concept of "deschooling." Where

[21]This is based upon a proposal my colleague Joel H. Spring and I submitted to the Department of Education at Case Western Reserve University in the spring of 1971.

possible, direct observation of alternative schools would be employed. Course treatment will include historical as well as current perspectives.

junior year

The design of new forms   1-year course   8–10 credit hours
Students would engage in the design of alternate forms of education at three different levels.

> **a**   The organization of the people: Who would be involved? In what roles? To accomplish what? With what sources of support?
>
> **b**   What would be learned? By whom? For what reason? How would instruction and learning take place? (This selection would draw upon an interdisciplinary team of consultants.)
>
> **c**   What would be the learning environment? What kinds of space? To do what? What kinds of equipment? To do what? What other resources needed?
> (This section would be assisted by faculty from the architecture and environmental-design programs.)

senior year

1   *Skills for new forms*   6–8 credit hours
This course would offer individualized instruction in specific teaching skills appropriate to the specific new form of education the student would hope to participate in upon graduation. A wide variety of skills training would be available, and when possible, real settings would be available for practice. When real settings were unavailable, simulation training would be attempted.

2   *Consequences of alternative forms*   3 credit hours
The examination of the expected social, political, economic, and psychological consequences of each of the alternative forms pro-

posed or designed. Although each student will approach his particular alternative individually, there would be comparative analysis of all forms.

Total credit hours 23–27

In addition, admission to the program will presume the demonstration, by more than just a list of courses taken, of a wide range of knowledge in the social sciences and humanities as well as in-depth knowledge of a specialty that is appropriate to the alternative form the student proposes to pursue.

The idealism latent in alternative forms reflects the importance young people recognize in education. In fact, some are awed by the teaching role, so sensitive are they to its potential for either good or evil. A student said to me, "We want to be really good teachers, but we really don't understand what that means. Like in Christianity, we all want to be like Christ, but we really don't know what it means to be a Christ." Clearly, traditional, mechanical training programs will not answer this student's concerns, and one can immediately understand such a student's reluctance to become enmeshed in the stifling complex organizational paraphernalia of many public school systems. Indeed, such a student must be recognized as having been liberated in the highest sense of our tradition of liberal education. And he intends, in all his idealism, to liberate all others. If Reich is correct, he intends to do so *by example* rather than by violence, although violence is always a temptation to the impatient, the supremely frustrated, and the revolutionary.

It seems possible to say that the consecutive culture is having a significant impact on schools. What Gross called "the radical's platform" is not so radical that whole school systems, as well as individual schools in and out of systems, are not attempting such reforms in part. A review of Gross's points assures us that:[22]

[22]Gross, op. cit.

1   The increasing popularity of the open classroom is a move toward making the student rather than the teacher the center of education. It is to be hoped that the open-classroom concept will not succumb to misunderstandings and misinterpretations as did the child-centered concept of an earlier period.

2   Schools today, here and there, now and then, are facing the issue of "artificial discipline, bureaucratic requirements and adults' rigid ideas about what children need to learn." More importantly, state departments of education, the United States Office of Education, the various accreditation agencies, and other policy groups have begun to respond to the need to liberate the child and his school. The USOE's proposed program of Teacher Renewal Centers could have a profound impact if properly implemented.

3   As school organizational structures are adjusted to better fit the task of education, the mechanical responses will be changed. Pace-setting high schools today have dropped dress codes, many of the compulsory attendance regulations, regularly assigned homework, and other such features in favor of more individual self-expression and responsibility. Uniform and competitive testing and rigid grading policies have been slower to change, since we in the universities have been reluctant to admit students without these trophies of achievement.

4   Textbooks will not change until the realities of the market change. Publishers have difficulty making a profit on texts that do not appeal to a mass market. However, the day of the uniform single text is passing, and it is only a matter of time until publishers revamp their procedures to meet the new demands.

5   Schools are responding to the demands of both students and parents for smaller size. The ill-fated Bundy plan in New York was the beginning of smaller units more directly accountable to parents. Other community participation plans also are moving toward more personal, intimate, and participatory organizational schemes. Large

165

high schools in some places have reorganized themselves into "houses" or subunits, which gives the student a sense of identity within the school's total structure. The institution "rediscovers" him in his house, his own administrative unit.

6 Certification requirements for teachers, per se, will probably not be abolished, since society will be reluctant to abandon licensure as a procedure, particularly in such a sensitive arena as education. Parents will continue to demand assurance that teachers are "qualified." But the definition of qualified is being modified. The schools without walls are demonstrating that learning can take place under the tutelage of people other than certified teachers. A society can, of course, use the certification issue as a weapon against alternative schools, as was done in San Francisco by school authorities to attack the free schools set up by Chinese parents who were resisting a school-integration busing plan. The issue will be the definition of certification rather than its continued existence.

7 The great testing mythology is already under attack, and compulsory testing, particularly "intelligence" testing, is now being reassessed in many quarters. Until such testing rids itself of the assumptions of a uniform best model, it will continue to be subjected to attacks, particularly from excluded groups. Entrance examinations too are under fire, but until the open-admissions experiments, such as the ones at the City University of New York and at many community colleges across the land, are carefully evaluated, it is probable that entrance requirements will remain. The entire prestige system upon which colleges and universities depend would be threatened if it was demonstrated that entrance requirements had little bearing upon subsequent performance.

8 Civil-rights groups will continue to apply pressure on tax-supported and tax-exempt colleges and universities to remove entrance requirements that imply a past experience exclusively in the Dick and Jane model.

9   As alternative schools grow, and if voucher plans are enacted that would enable such schools to survive financially, then legal barriers will relax. It is unrealistic, however, to expect any society to abolish all requirements and restrictions placed upon the process of educating its young. Neither does it seem likely that any society will abandon the process of schooling, as Ivan Illich suggests. In highly complex and organized societies, education will not be left to chance, and like other activities, it will be organized. The more pertinent question is *how*.

10   When the many intricate problems of a voucher plan are confronted, it seems visionary to expect its adoption in the immediate future. The voucher system is not particularly radical when viewed as an extension of a market economy, but it is radical if applied to a social institution that at least claims not to operate on market principles. Public education, in principle, is supported by all for all with a considerable verbal commitment to provide its services on an equal basis. The voucher plan offers the consumer a chance to select his own kind of educational experience and probably his own level of quality. It is not clear how this could operate effectively, any more than it is clear how a consumer of judicial services could select the court of his choice or the consumer of welfare could select the welfare agency of his choice. The voucher plan does, however, offer an alternative to allocating increasing public resources to unresponsive systems that offer poor-quality services.

        It would appear that the most likely and the most efficient plan of alternatives would be for enlightened school systems to so organize that they are able to offer meaningful alternatives to their clientele within the public school framework. Berkeley, California, proposes this course, for one example. Philadelphia and Chicago have done so with the creation of their Parkway and Metro schools. The danger, of course, is that alternatives *within* a system may turn out to be no alternatives at all, but merely public-relations gimmicks designed to placate challenging critics. These schemes might stall reform for a time, but students, particularly consecutive-culture students, require that reality not only *look* real, but also *feel* real. They would soon unmask such diversions.

Perhaps the way school systems can avoid censure from those who demand that schools remain traditional, coercive, and excessively tied to place and structure is to offer alternatives that do not look like alternatives. With employment of computerized modular scheduling, liberal use of independent-study programs, and school organization by vertical age groupings, the only tradition remaining is the grade system, which, of course, given the other reforms, is a meaningless but perhaps necessary gesture to the old guard. The elementary structure will be much more difficult to disguise, although schools have sometimes been able to persuade their patrons that nongraded schools and open classrooms are chic.

In urban schools, the answer to the question of social support and rapport lies in the involvement of the community itself in the institution of the school. Urban parents, often products of poor urban schools, have not yet lost faith in education, even if they are suspicious of the present forms of schooling. If they see excitement in their children, if they themselves have successes in occasional forays back into the educational world, and if they feel they have something to say about what happens in schools, it is possible that their negative, and ofttimes hostile, feelings toward schools will change and legitimate experimentation will be supported.

Consecutive-culture young people who work in urban schools have repeatedly demonstrated that they like the urban child. They are not afraid to show their affection, and they are unimpressed by rules of social distance. They are then a powerful potential force to woo back the loyalty of urban parents. If consecutive-culture young people who proclaim that they care about urban children and their parents (and the social, economic, and political conditions in which they live) can channel that care into any kind of a positive, sustained effort, urban schools may indeed become more than a daily drudgery.

chapter seven

forecasting
the issues

The educational sociologist, as a monitor and interpreter of the interpenetrations of schools and society, is often called upon to forecast the future of those relationships. It is to be hoped that the educational sociologist will make use of the theory, methodology, and data of sociology in arriving at such judgments. He must, however, apply his resources to the realities of education.

Methodologically, demography can be an important tool. Socialization theory, particularly as it deals with the building of political behavior, is also of special interest today. Finally, what is happening in the "profession" may predict future trends in public education. There may be other areas that are important to social forecasting, but I shall deal only with demography, political socialization, and professionalism, each discussed separately and with no particular order or importance implied.

"Demography is the study of the size, territorial distribution, and composition of population, changes therein, and the components of such changes, which may be identified as natality (births), mortality (deaths), territorial movement (migration) and social mobility (change of status)."[1]

This definition may seem somewhat restrictive to the educational sociologist, but it is understandably so because it was designed to be useful to sociologists in the context of their concerns for theories of social structure and social mobility. It is possible, however, to construct a broader definition. One could consider demography as the total study of "people factors," which would include a variety of measures of "people activity" (class data as opposed to individual). The educational sociologist whose interest and intent is to use these materials to solve educational problems rather than to build sociological theory can be more expansive, since he needs to know a great deal about demography (broadly defined) and human ecology as he supplies "people-factor" data to the schools, and they in turn plan and execute appropriate educational programs, plan their services to and with the community, and monitor the society that supports them.

What comes to mind immediately is, of course, the need for hard data with which a school can project enrollments, or estimate voter behavior patterns on school tax issues, or check socioeconomic status and needs, or even detect the presence of any distinctive ethnic or racial populations. Such practical uses of demographic data do not necessarily need any elaborate supportive theory to be valid.

[1]Philip M. Hauser and Otis Dudley Duncan, quoted in Leo F. Schnore, *The Urban Scene,* Free Press, New York, 1965, p. 50.

The primary sources of demographic data are: (1) Censuslike enumerations; (2) registrations of events of significant interest (vital statistics such as births, deaths, and marriages); and (3) special inventories such as economic activity measures, prices, employment, income surveys, property status, or household data.

There are problems with all of these sources that make it difficult for the educational sociologist to function as a persistent monitor. The United States census, for example, is only taken once every ten years; it can become out-of-date and useless if an area is experiencing high mobility or the need is for extremely current data. For example, the initial allocations of funds from the Elementary and Secondary Education Act of 1965 were based upon 1960 census data. In high-mobility states like California, Oregon, Washington, Arizona, and Florida, the 1960 data was inaccurate in 1965. School districts that had significant poverty populations in 1960 may have had virtually none in 1965, which would invalidate their claim to the alloted funds. Conversely, school districts that had little or no poverty populations in 1960 may have found by 1965 significant numbers of poor, but no allocation of ESEA funds. Two conclusions are possible: (1) One should not expect United States census data to be useful for solutions to immediate, short-range problems; or (2) the Census Bureau must consider expanding its operation so that interim or special censuses on important variables can be carried out more often than once every ten years.

For the educational sociologist to be able to present a total picture of what is happening to a given population, he must gather data from a variety of sources. There is no single source available in most places, although some regional planning agencies are attempting to create data banks that draw on all available informational sources. However, a number of problems emerge from this effort. Each agency that collects data does so to meet its peculiar needs and purposes. The form in which the data is collected is designed to those needs-purposes specifications. In other words, there is no uniformity of form. Collection agencies may also be dealing with different jurisdictions, resulting in different spatial units. For example, data may be collected concerning a city, a school district, a congressional district, a ward, a special-purpose district (sewer, water, etc.), a county, or even a region, none of which have precisely the same boundaries. In the case of still smaller units, school attendance areas rarely coincide, for example, with either census tracts or voting precincts.

Another problem arises when the educational sociologist realizes that some collection agencies deliberately distort data for their own political purposes. The distortions might be made to assure the agency's continuing good reputation for productivity, or they might be employed to gain a larger appropriation in the next budget. Rarely are there laws that (1) insist upon the submission of data or cooperation among data-gathering agencies, and (2) authorize periodic audits of the accuracy of the data published. Some school districts I have known, for example, have been guilty of deliberately distorting their dropout rates, or their absentee rates, or other mobility measures. These actions often stem from a desire to appear as a stable district, or to maintain per capita state financial aid, or simply to avoid the criticism a high dropout rate might generate.

The ESEA program was geared to poverty populations, but income data is viewed by some as private, and school districts were hard pressed to obtain the necessary figures without invading that privacy. For a time, social policy also forbade the collection of data that differentiated people by race, but this was changed because it proved dysfunctional in the solving of problems that the original policy was supposed to help eradicate. A school district, for example, could not achieve racial balance if the law forbade the keeping of statistics on the racial distribution of its student population.

The use of demography to collect data that may make it possible to predict problems before they arrive with all their special urgencies has not been exercised by many urban agencies, including schools. Highway planners, for example, need to know whom they are displacing, particularly in a city, and what is likely to happen to those so displaced. This knowledge, acquired in advance, could help avoid many problems and human miseries. Before I built a school, which might have to last some fifty years, I would want to know more than just how many pupils live in the area. Who are the pupils? Are there any mobility trends among them? What is happening to the neighborhood (trends)? What other agencies have plans for the area? What is the age distribution in the population, with particular attention to childbearing couples? Has density increased or decreased? Why? Armed with the answers to these and other questions, I could evaluate my investment in a new school.

Demographic factors are not necessarily causative in any one-to-one sense. Data needs interpretation and even additional study. For example, the school knows that it is experiencing a dropping enrollment. Why? Is it movement away from the district? Or are the families growing older and passing the peak of childbearing? Is there a lower birthrate? Is the problem economic, political, social, or what? Demographic studies of the area can often uncover the reasons for a change, and they may not be the reasons expected. I recall a case where the school burned down and the district declined to rebuild in that area because they had figures that showed a declining enrollment. The community, on the other hand, knew that ground would soon be broken for a huge, public-housing development and argued for a new school on the old site. School officials had been unaware of the new public housing (lack of interagency communication), but the community people were unaware that the public-housing units were going to be designed for the elderly. In other words, neither had proper data.

Any attempts to install a voucher system, or to predict parochial-school erosion of public-school attendance (or vice versa), or to plan the future on the basis of the tax base, should be made with accurate demographic data. Schools that embrace multicultural, multiracial education will find demographic data imperative. In fact, any school planning that is premised upon "people factors" and "people activity" must use demography if the planning is to be useful and successful. Similarly, school districts could use demography to study what impact their decisions have had upon the population. Evaluation may be as important as planning; it can check the validity of the planning as well as isolate new problems.

Philip M. Hauser's analysis of the early figures from the 1970 census[2] reveals a number of facts that could have great significance for educators. His conclusions are mostly national, although some are by region and state and some by metropolitan areas. Each bit of information needs to be interpreted in the light of local variables.

Some of Hauser's findings are, as I read them:

1 The West and South continue to have the greatest growth.

2 California and Florida had the greatest increases, but Nevada had the highest percentage (71 percent).

3 West Virginia and North and South Dakota experienced the greatest declines.

4 The increase in the population was concentrated in 25 percent of the nation's counties. In other words, the last ten-year period reflects massive metropolitanization, as urban life swallowed up the equivalent of the nation's entire population increase, 24 million persons.

5 The nation's population is now 73.5 percent urban, in the West 82.9 percent, the Northeast 80.4 percent, the North Central area 71.6 percent, and the South 64.6 percent.

[2]Philip M. Hauser, "The Census of 1970," *Scientific American,* vol. 225, no. 1, July 1971.

6   The central cities, however, tell a different story. Of the top twenty-five in 1960, twelve lost population. Four (Detroit, Cleveland, St. Louis, and Pittsburgh) lost more than 10 percent .

7   However, of the fifty leading metropolitan areas, all but one grew. Two hundred forty-three Standard Metropolitan Statistical Areas (SMSA) absorbed 84 percent of the nation's growth.

8   For the first time, the suburban populations outnumbered the city populations.

9   The black population increased at almost double the rate of the white population (20.1 percent to 11.8 percent). The "out-migration" of blacks from the South continued, but at a slower pace. Blacks, however, were still greater in percentage of population in the South than any other region.

10   The movement of blacks continued to be to the central cities regardless of region. Washington, D.C., Newark, Gary, and Atlanta all had black populations in excess of 50 percent. Detroit, St. Louis, Baltimore, New Orleans, Wilmington, Birmingham, and Richmond, Virginia, all had black populations in excess of 40 percent.

11   The black increases in the cities were only partly due to the exodus of whites. Incidentally, blacks also gained in large percentages in the suburbs, even though these gains still represented relatively small numbers.

Hauser concluded that there were some discernible trends in the structure of the population too.

1   There is a long-time trend toward smaller families and smaller household units. Family size decreased slightly (from 3.65 to 3.57), but there was also an increase in the number of both young and old living apart ("undoubling" or establishing separate homes).

2   Nonfamily households showed a 49.3 percent increase. (These are households either of one person or of two or more unrelated persons living together.)

Perhaps the most significant findings for school people are the changes in the age structure and birthrate. Hauser's analysis could abruptly demolish some currently growing myths and should alert school planners to what lies ahead.

1   There was a 44.3 percent increase in the group of persons aged 15–19.

2   There was a 51.6 percent increase in the group of persons aged 20–24.

3   Thus, the late teen-age and young-adult populations together represent nearly 50 percent of the decade's total increase.

4   These combined groups represent a childbearing group of great significance. The 1968 birthrate started up again, and in 1969, birthrates increased in forty-three of the fifty states.

5   *These findings are predictive of another baby boom that will occur when these products of the post-World War II baby boom arrive at childbearing age. The first waves of this boom should hit the schools in the late 1970s and continue on into the 1980s.*

Current surpluses of teachers (which may be the function of lack of school finances rather than lack of children) may again be shortages in the not too distant future. The decline in teacher-education enrollments currently being experienced in many colleges and universities will have to be reversed, since a college student enrolling in 1973 will not finish until 1977 (under normal circumstances), and the boom may have already begun by then. Early-childhood–education activities, such as preschool, Head Start, or nursery schools will, of course, feel this boom sooner. If the population is growing more urban, the new baby boom is obviously going to be felt there with greatest intensity. Data concerning family size according to racial or socioeconomic status is not yet available, so one should not speculate on how the baby boom will be spatially distributed in metropolitan areas.

Hauser also reports that the number of people over sixty-five years old also increased at a high rate, though not as fast as in the previous decade. Senior citizens now represent 10 percent of the total population. This is important to school districts that must confront voters with financial issues. Older people tend to vote against increasing taxes since they are often living on fixed retirement incomes and any tax increase represents to them a corresponding decline in their standard of living. States with large retired populations (the Sun Belt) have felt the impact of this reality for some time, and some have had to lower the percentage of votes needed to assure passage of financial issues to account for the "automatic" negative votes of senior citizens. Recent court decisions attacking the property tax as the primary resource for school monies may help older people who often have property, but do not often have cash.

School districts that may have to respond to recent court orders to reorganize to achieve equal tax loads or integration can call for extensive help from the National Center for Educational Statistics in the U.S. Office of Education. In late 1971, the center announced that school district population maps, based upon 1970 census data, would be available on microfilm for some 9,000 districts with enrollments of 300 or more. In addition, twenty-one major school administrative areas are available. It is planned that the center will also make available additional data from the 1970 Census of Population and Housing.

Such data as is being offered by the center could be a major aid to educational planners. It also represents governmental recognition of the need for demographic data for schools. The most extensive use of this resource will, of course, be by school jurisdictions that have access to the services of professional demographers or educational sociologists who have had training in demography. The former will be specialized enough to read and process the data on the maps, but the educational sociologist should have the additional skills to interpret the data to solve educational problems and to carry out the functions of monitoring, interpreting, and forecasting.

Socialization is a process common to all organized societies. Its intent is to teach and to provide the opportunity to learn the ways of a society, the behavior expected by the society as well as the behavior frowned upon. It is inevitably a selective process because no society can expect to control all behavior, and some, particularly democracies, disdain any desire to do so. In a democracy, it is argued, the socialization process should promote norms of behavior and attempt to ensure individual fulfillment at the same time. Induction into the society then should be a sensitive process, compulsory only when it is absolutely necessary to the maintenance of the society, and stimulating, to assure the dynamic creativity that, it is asserted, is the hallmark of a free people.

The process of education, as it is formalized in organized schooling, is a central force in the socialization process in American society. It is central because: (1) As the society becomes increasingly sophisticated and complex, socialization agents such as the family have difficulty dealing with the multiplicity of issues; and (2) as knowledge expands, the schools become the primary access route to whatever good things the society has to offer. Such rewards include social or political power and control. Historically we see that:

> . . . There is an intimate relationship between education and social control. The man who was educated was the man who possessed vitally needed skills, and the man who possessed the needed skills was soon the man of power. . . . Thus men in power in societies recognized early that a substantial portion of their power rested upon their possession of the fruits of educa-

tion, and history will record their reaction to this insight. Men in power, wanting to perpetuate that power and the privileges which accompanied it, began to limit access of education to all those outside their power group. By limiting access to education, they automatically limited access to power to the ruling class, to the priesthood, or whatever group possessed final power in a particular society.[3]

When almost universal public education became a cornerstone of American society, access to education was still limited for some groups (see Chapter Three), but the new strategy was to control education's input into the socialization process. In other words, if who would get education could not be limited, the *kind* of education they got could be. In effect, the educational input could be controlled so that a socialization favorable to the maintenance of existent power arrangements could be produced. There will be many who will call this process indoctrination and mean by it a pejorative and undemocratic process. However, it has always been difficult to distinguish the fine line between legitimate socialization and indoctrination. For example, is teaching kindergarten children the pledge of allegiance to the flag (in words they do not understand) an act of reasonable socialization or flagrant indoctrination? There are probably a score of different value positions that would give as many different answers to such a question.

Paul Goodman asserts that the whole procedure of socialization has now become "processing."[4] He implies that this is an extremely dehumanized, impersonal affair that is unnecessary and a gross affront to freedom. Along with the corporate single-product-model concept, the aim has been to police youth for the

---

[3]Louis Fischer and Donald R. Thomas, *Social Foundation of Educational Decisions,* Wadsworth, Belmont, Calif., 1965, pp. 35–36. With permission.
[4]Paul Goodman, "No Processing Whatever," in Ronald Gross and Beatrice Gross (eds.), *Radical School Reform,* Simon & Schuster, New York, 1969, p. 98.

period of time they are involved with the formal socialization process (schooling); and that period is defined as the time during which it is necessary to keep youth off the labor market in the interests of a sound economy. "The results of these efforts have been further to build the power of the school colony within the community as a central place for teaching what the corporation needs . . . a sense of hierarchy, competition, and submissiveness."[5]

Goodman submits the notion that there should be no formal processing whatsoever. If he means to equate processing with socialization, one might suspect that his vision is impaired. All societies in all times, in order to sustain themselves, have engaged in some form of socialization, and there is no readily available evidence that suggests that this is about to change. The real question is not whether there will be socialization, but rather: How much and what kind?

Robert Hess, a leading educational researcher in the field of political socialization, suggests that the schools have badly mishandled the aspect of the socialization process that introduces America's political system to young people.

> The increasing volume of protest reflects the new realism: Young people no longer find either government action or social and economic reality congruent with the national ideology and rhetoric of morality, civil rights, equality of opportunity, or desire for peace. *It is not these values themselves that are under attack,* but the failure of representatives of the society to recognize the disparity between ideals and reality and take some appropriate action.[6] (Italics added.)

Hess's argument is that "the schools have contributed to

[5]Marcus Raskin, "Discussion," *Harvard Educational Review,* vol. 38, no. 3, p. 550, Summer 1968.
[6]Robert Hess, "Political Socialization in the Schools," *Harvard Educational Review,* vol. 38, no. 3, p. 530, Summer 1968. With permission. Italics added to emphasize the acceptance of the assumption that schools have indeed taught the ideal, even if they have not taught the reality. Between these, says the poet T. S. Eliot, falls the shadow.

divisions within society by teaching a view of the nation and its political processes which is incomplete and simplistic, stressing values and ideals but ignoring social realities."[7] This may be both an unintentional and a deliberate oversight on the part of schools. If, in fact, the "teaching of social and political interaction omits both the components of emotion and of action, *the two elements that are most likely to effect change,*"[8] (italics added) we can begin to see causes for the public schools' apparent inattentiveness.

To insert emotion and action into the political-socialization process would be to assure controversy, and no word in the history of American education is more likely to terrorize the public schoolmaster than the word *controversy*. Reckless public educators who attempted to teach critical thinking or to espouse open inquiry in the classroom know the public wrath such activities can engender. In other words, there are some topics and some activities that the society does not deem appropriate for the schools. It should be clear that those topics and activities that seem to threaten or oppose the current political, social, and economic power structure are most offensive, and the power structure has the means to assure itself that it will not be offended, particularly by public "servants" such as educators.

The dilemma of American education is then unequivocal. Assigned the task of socialization, the educator is enjoined to complete it without threatening or opposing any powerful forces in the society. If he processes students in order to avoid controversy, he is criticized by Goodman or a hundred other advocates of educational freedom. If he liberates students, he is usually subject to immediate retaliation from the power structure. The choice of no processing versus more processing is hardly a happy set of alternatives. Schoolmen have attempted to straddle the dilemma by teaching the ideals of democracy didactically, avoiding emotion and

[7]Ibid., p. 531.
[8]Ibid., p. 534.

action, but insisting upon repeated assurances from students that they do indeed understand the ideals and values and mean to live by them even if the school cannot provide them an arena for practice. If Hess's analysis is correct, schoolmen have evidently been reasonably successful in this endeavor. It is now the society's turn to act on the disparities that students, so educated, have detected.

The dilemma that society faces is also clear-cut. If protesting students are to be reconciled, then the socialization process must be modified to include emotion and action. Hess suggests:

> Perhaps the most significant objective now is to teach involvement and understanding, using experiences which combine action and feeling with ideas of how a complex political and bureaucratic system works. Such an approach should:
>
> 1) be candid and explicit about social and political realities and disagreements;
>
> 2) emphasize both psychological and structural (sociological) processes such as the role of anger and hate in race relations, and how institutions have contributed to racism inadvertently and deliberately;
>
> 3) provide channels for effective change and action—a knowledge of how the system works and how it may be influenced.[9]

The alternative to better and more realistic socialization is more repressive processing. This might take the form of diluting or even eliminating the teaching of democratic ideals except at a bare slogan level. It is doubtful that this is reasonable, since the society would already have to be well on the way to being a police state to tolerate such actions. Besides, the current generation is too filled with itself and its mission to allow it. Continuation along the current

[9]Ibid., p. 535. With permission.

path—teaching of forms, ideals, and values devoid of emotion and action—is another approach, but that may only increase the tempo of present activity of the young and the minority-group activists who are demanding an end to the disparities between the ideal and the real. If one cannot create ignorance and apathy and one cannot continue to teach ideals without reality, then the only other alternative seems to be outright suppression. If that is the choice—and some radical thinkers feel that such a choice has already been made—then the purpose of socialization has already been compromised. Repression would amount to a Catch-22 kind of argument that the only way a democratic society can be saved or maintained is to stamp it out. I hope it is clear that some people actually agree with this latter argument.

I must, however, return to the notion that democracy and freedom need not be feared by the average citizen or the teacher. Earl Kelley has summed it up.

> The questioning of the advisability of teaching current, and hence, controversial issues is based on a concept of the denial of freedom. When the teacher abandons the idea that he alone is going to choose what is to be learned, the problem disappears. The learning which ensues when learners are consulted is mostly controversial in some degree, because it is largely current. Settled matters are studied as they are apropos to current issues. The teacher then becomes the facilitator of learning and a defender of freedom. This is a fine role for anyone teaching in a democracy.[10]

The forecast in this area is, of course, continued controversy. However, that in itself reassures us that the change process is at work. Educators will either move toward more effective (realistic) political socialization, thereby generating action that will cause change, or they will continue to skirt the issue by teaching only the

---

[10]Earl C. Kelley, "The Teaching of Controversial Issues," *Review of General Semantics,* vol. 19, no. 2, p. 147, July 1962. With permission.

ideals and values. If present trends persist, this will cause anger in and protest from the young when they do confront reality, which will create pressure for change as it is currently doing. The problem for the power structure then will be either to openly repress or to create mechanisms within the system that give the appearance of allowing change without really changing the basic power distribution.

Radical youth and militants among the minority groups tend to reject the "work within the system for change" line of thought. They point out that the system is so arranged as to make real change impossible. For them, the political-socialization process must lead to a fundamental revolution that sweeps away most of the framework within which we now operate our society. Basically, they approach the problem by implicitly redefining democracy as something nearer to anarchy or a form of state authoritarianism directed in behalf of the people. Again we are faced with the reasoning that the way to save democracy is to destroy democracy.

In my judgment the issue will not be resolved in favor of either extreme, although I sense more danger from the repression alternative than I do from the alternatives proposed by radical youth. I do forecast change as the younger vision of democracy reaches its peak of political influence, and the demographic data we have just reviewed indicates that that time is not far off.

Professionalism is a dream hard to forget. It is also hard to reexamine. The siren songs of educational leaders who demand it are old but still appealing. The issue lingers on, repeated in ancient refrains and chants, but never quite confronts the uncomfortable questions raised by Myron Lieberman in 1956.[11] Education has not resolved the issue of function, the problem of authority, the issue of autonomy (and, therefore, the issue of responsibility and accountability), or the dilemmas of ethics. It was Lieberman's contention "that the overwhelming majority of educators in service have

---

[11] Myron Lieberman, *Education as a Profession,* Prentice-Hall, Englewood Cliffs, N.J., 1956.

never been exposed to a rigorous analysis of the problems of professionalizing education."[12] This is probably still true, because the National Education Association trudges on shrilly insisting that education is a profession because they say so, while the American Federation of Teachers issues "no comment" statements, and the American Association of University Professors hardly interrupts the polite taking of its toast and tea. NEA states:

> The teaching profession wants to and must assume responsibility and accountability for its own destiny. The profession is ready and able to govern itself. What is lacking is the legal authorization to do so.
>
> It is proposed that there be established in each state a teaching Practices Commission, composed of practitioners with the authority to accredit institutions which prepare teachers; to issue, suspend, revoke, and reinstate certificates; to establish standards of professional practice and ethics; and to promote studies and research to improve teacher education, including initial, graduate, and continuing education. Through such a Commission the teaching profession could govern itself. Until the teaching profession is delegated by state legislation the right to govern itself, the profession cannot be held fully responsible or accountable.[13]

Of course the notion that public educators cannot be held responsible or accountable until the public grants them the broad powers involved in autonomy is nonsense. Because the public, via its legislatures, is holding educators accountable for the present state of education is precisely the reason it will not extend the educator's power. The dysfunctionalism of urban education is not the product of the NAACP, CORE, the Mexican American Political

[12]Ibid., p. viii.
[13]Working paper of the Joint Project on Professional Autonomy, National Education Association, Washington, D.C., November 1969. With permission.

Association, or any other such group. With at least the complicity of educators, intentionally or unintentionally, it is the product of maintaining educational systems that educators surely must have detected were failing their clients. Even certification has not proven it provides either expertise or good teaching. Indeed, the rigidity of certification in most states has tended to frustrate rather than enhance educational practice. Alternative schools are proving all too often that accreditation, certification, standards of practice, and ethics become distorted when played through the suffocating intransigence of complex urban school organizations. It is certainly not the function of a profession to concur in such distortions of the educational process. Possibly such an indictment is too brutal, but it is a reality.

The public is more likely to see and hear organized educators working for goals that are fundamentally self-serving.

David D. Darland states, for example:

> Teachers have at least three major areas of concern: (1) the concerns of being an employed person, (2) concerns unique to being a professional, and (3) concerns related to teaching in a subject area, level, or specialty:
>
> . . . The first area . . . includes economic and personal concerns; the second relates to standards, professional development, rights and responsibility; and the third relates to curriculum and instructional matters.[14]

The public, urban people in particular, would probably have appreciated *equal* concern being expressed for their children or, for that matter, anyone's children, since the client-serving function of education is a paramount issue to them.

[14]D. D. Darland, "TEPS in Action," Tentative draft for the 1969-70 Regional Teacher Education and Professional Standards Conference, National Education Association, Washington, D.C., December 1969, January 1970. With permission.

This is not to say that salary and working conditions are inconsequential matters. Educators have been exploited for too many years to deny their legitimate claims for adequate pay and reasonable working conditions. But now it is a matter of public concern that that seems to be all they talk about. While it may be right and justified for trade unions—organized to attack precisely these problems—it may seem inappropriate as the apparent central concern of a professional organization.

It is also true that teachers are part of a "new class" referred to by Gus Tyler.

> Teachers are a symbol and surrogate of the various elements that have been emerging in the economy since 1950. They are white collar, publicly-employed professionals, providing a service. They are also numerous, articulate and in fields with a tradition of collective action. The teachers—like police, firemen and social workers—are irked by the demeaning disparity between their alleged social role and their actual social status, between what is asked of them and what is given unto them. They are expected to manage a multitude of social complexes, playing the ancestral role of the "priesthood," while being relegated in status to the ranks of the proletariat.[15]

Nevertheless, professionalism is an achieved status, not ascribed. Even though the demands on teachers are great, it is their *performance* that earns or does not earn professional status.

The resistance of school authorities to meeting public demands for an education that is more functional and less authoritarian is, then, still another obstacle to professionalization. I am, of course, assuming that educators can and will eventually define their goals in concert with the public, so that clear-cut directions are available. Darland seems to echo this in another

---

[15]Gus Tyler, "The Faculty Joins the Proletariat," *Change,* vol. 3, no. 8, p. 42, Winter 1971/1972. With permission.

publication when he says: "For unless the profession can put its own house in order, clarify its own sense of direction, and establish its own policies and procedures, it will be ineffective in working with the public and its own members."[16]

There is little doubt that one of the problems of putting the house in order emerges from excessive new-class concern for unionlike activities.

> The attention of teachers is easily diverted to the support of a professional organization as an end in itself. Jurisdictional conflicts are thus created. The organization becomes the end, and the internecine conflict among organizations consumes the energy and displaces constructive programs needed for development of an effective profession.[17]

The welfare issue also arose from the frustration that educators experienced in dealing with corporation-oriented school boards and superintendents. The early success of the teacher unions stimulated a competition for collective-bargaining rights among the various educational organizations. When these organizations appeared to succeed (and, for the first time, had "muscle" and reveled in the new-found opportunity to exert it), professional self-determination seemed to gain credibility. It was a privatistic vision, however, in a *public* sector. At once it both spurred and defeated the claim to professionalism, in that it proved that educators operating as collective bargaining units, could exert power, but it also caused the public to shift from its traditional view of educators as white-collar to a new view that saw educators as just another blue-collar group competing in the mad pursuit of material goals. It also seemed to contradict some public statements by educational leaders that

[16]D. D. Darland, "Preparation in the Governance of the Profession," *Teachers for the Real World,* American Association of Colleges for Teacher Education, Washington, D.C., 1969, p. 135. With permission.
[17]Ibid., p. 137. With permission.

they were truly supportive of increased parental and student control of schools. What powers would be left available to parents and students if the professionals controlled licensure, working conditions, curriculum and instruction, and most personnel decisions was not made clear. The Ocean Hill-Brownsville dispute in New York City was fought precisely over many of the issues involved in the question of who should own the power.

A new pull for change, emerging from the minority communities, the youth culture, and the resurgence of radical reappraisal, now confronts the profession. The new thrust is highly individualistic rather than organizational and has spawned hundreds of alternative schools that are *in direct competition* with the established profession and established schools. Multidisciplinary training too has begun to break the monopoly of an educational establishment that had always insisted upon exclusive control of initial, graduate, continuing teacher, and administrator education. There has even been the suggestion that educational organizations, at least in their present form and with their present leadership, are irrelevant to the monstrous tasks of rejuvenating public education.

The central argument now emerges as a choice between *stagnation* and *transition*. In stagnation, the teacher will remain *organizational*. Such a teacher is status-oriented and traditional in her assumptions that: (1) Learning is almost solely the consequence of teaching; (2) schools should perpetuate the social-assimilation model, i.e., Dick and Jane; (3) the curriculum must be sequential according to age and grade; (4) the learning environment needs to be restricted to a closed and fixed space; and (5) the first concern of teachers should be their own personal welfare.

In transition, the teacher will become *humanistic*. She is prepared to admit without being threatened that most learning takes place independently of her direct teaching, and she is comfortable with a new role that is free, individualistic, unafraid, open, creative, noncompetitive, and warmly interpersonal. She respects children and celebrates their individuality and their personal dignity. Learning, she recognizes, is independent of props; the physical environment need not dominate, any more than all content and organization need be structured by authority. Teaching is an art, wedded to the discipline of social-science methodology.

Stagnation offers only the hollow echoes of old arguments that parents and students really do not care about anymore. It has always depended upon internal control rather than vision and activism. Stagnation offers tired arrangements, replete with rambling and irrelevant slogans, which communicate to the public an absence of dynamism and much more dedication to creature comforts than to performance. Is it not obvious that public discussion about experimentation with performance contracting in schools is a clear sign that current performance is perceived as deficient? The society is saying, as the mother in Watts did, that schools should do what they are supposed to do. Many noneducators (rightfully) cannot tell the schools precisely how to do their job, but they can and do insist that their children be educated.

Transition, on the other hand, offers, to use Reich's word, a "greening" of American education. It offers the chance to move toward: (1) An affective thrust of personal commitment; (2) the excitement of creating new structures; (3) the achievement of personal fulfillment for both teacher and learner; and (4) a higher plane of what George Leonard has called "ecstasy."[18] This is not solely glandular; it has intellectual integrity and a sense of realism about the delivery of services to children.

Realistically, though, I must admit that the old ways and the old organizations may not be capable of changing. There are so many vested interests that would have to yield: Political, economic, even personal. When the old National Football League felt its arteries hardening and its pace slowing, it took the challenge of the young American Football League to stir the blood again. Perhaps then we

---

[18]George B. Leonard, *Education and Ecstasy,* Delacorte (Dell), New York, 1968.

need an American Education Association or an Alternative Education Association. As organizations for the future, they could capture with their vitality and vision the imagination of the young—both as students and teachers—and regain the respect of the community—both as parents and patrons. Such an achievement might even lead to the capture of the elusive goal of professionalism, recognized by both practitioners and public.

I cannot legitimately forecast that these new possibilities will come to pass. However, I can predict the struggle, for it has already begun. The outcome is uncertain, but the contest is joined.

chapter eight
does reform
have a future?

There have been only two significant reform movements in the history of American education. A third is struggling to be born in the 1970s. There are exploratory studies of the first two: Michael Katz's *The Irony of Early School Reform* chronicles the first, which occurred in the mid nineteenth century; and Lawrence Cremin's award-winning *The Transformation of the School* describes the second, which took place in the early twentieth century.[1] Both

[1]Michael B. Katz, *The Irony of Early School Reform,* Beacon Press, Boston, 1970; and Lawrence A. Cremin, *The Transformation of the School,* Knopf, New York, 1961.

studies are attentive and are recognized for their excellent historiography, and both point to the same conclusion: In each instance, reform did not really occur. Assuming that reform is an appropriate activity in education, the educational sociologist needs to review why past reforms failed, lest embryonic contemporary reform movements be frustrated in the same way.

Let me clarify the language of this discussion at the outset. Used precisely, the word *reform* means to improve something by casting out the wrong or corrupt in it. In other words, reform is not simply change. The word *innovate* means to introduce something new or different; it is additive and does not necessarily imply either a housecleaning or even a replacement. Within this definition of *reform*, I used evaluative terms like *improve, wrong,* and *corrupt,* thus recognizing that there is a value setting into which such terms may be arranged. Reform movements always seem to have clear value positions and ample moral certitude. They know either what they do not like or what they want, but they rarely coordinate the two.

Katz reports that the early reform movement was directed, among other things, toward the improvement of the working class (a broad classification at best), but always in such a way that the power position of the social and economic elite was undisturbed. He states that reformers harangued the child and the parent from the lower classes with: "You are vicious, immoral, short-sighted and thoroughly wrong about most things. We are right; we shall show you the truth."[2] The reformers claimed to be seeking a new, enlightened, democratic society, one in which education was a joy to all, social progress was as inherent as moral goodness, and all citizens would be disciplined and informed and make appropriate contributions to the ultimate betterment of society. Educational reform was then a method of social reform.

The life of Horace Mann and the accounts of his frustrations perhaps best illustrate both the thrust of this early reform

[2]Katz, ibid., p. 215. Echoes of this somewhat colonialist position are heard today in reference to inner-city people, minority groups, and the rural poor.

movement and also its eventual inefficacy. Rather than reforming social systems, Mann wanted to reform people by having education transmit only the most lofty ideals of a true, Christian democracy. What Mann never understood was that his cultural transmission meant transmission of a *total social system* and therefore the transmission of the *same* power arrangements that currently prevailed in society and its institutions. Further, he apparently could not comprehend the idea that most of the reforms he sought were inimical to those power arrangements. The early twentieth-century reform, described by Cremin, confronted the same problem. Every effort to achieve the reformer's version of social and educational justice seemed to be undermined, attacked, and countered by those power interests whose position would be most threatened by the success of the reform. Our present reform movement is already facing the same adversaries, particularly as it stresses greater access for the poor to the material fruits of society, which means an adjustment in the stratification system and perhaps a redistribution of power.

> . . . In our society, as in others, we find that there are influential men at the head of important institutions who cannot afford to be found wrong, who find change inconvenient, perhaps intolerable, and who have financial or political interests they must conserve at any cost. Such men are, therefore, threatened in many respects by the theory of the democratic process and the concept of an ever-renewing society.[3]

We must repeat that there are also organizational and personal interests within the institution of education that are deterrents to reform. These people too are dedicated to maintenance rather than change, particularly if the change implies reform. Of course, such vested interests exist in every stratum of our society. In

[3]Neil Postman and Charles Weingartner, *Teaching as a Subversive Activity,* Delacorte Press (Dell), New York, 1969, p. 2. With permission.

short, American education, in its role as a cultural-transmission agent, has always been plagued by conflicts between maintenance agents and reformers. It is my contention that the reformers have lost out rather consistently, and for the rather obvious sociological reason that they have failed to confront the realities of the inertia in all social structures, the forces within any system that act to counterbalance its dynamic qualities.

Reform was in the air in the mid nineteenth century; it was the intoxicant of the dreamers and schemers who followed some "great inward Commander," to use Ralph Waldo Emerson's description of the participants of the Chardon Street Convention of 1840, called by the Friends of Universal Reform. "I wish to offer to your consideration some thoughts on the particular and general relations of man as a reformer . . . and a general inquisition into abuses," said Emerson.[4] Each reformer present, of course, had his own private visions. Those were the days of John Humphrey Noyes and his Oneida Perfectionists, Frances Wright and her Free-Inquirers, the early Mormons, Sylvester Graham of cracker fame, and Samuel Thomson, the enemy of Epsom salts. It was also the time of Horace Mann, America's earliest giant in education, who proclaimed:

> If I can be the means of ascertaining what is the best construction of school houses, what are the best books, what is the best mode of instruction; if I can discover by what appliance of means a non-thinking, non-reflecting, non-speaking child can most surely be trained into a noble citizen, ready to contend for the right, and to die for the right; if I can only obtain and diffuse throughout the state a few good ideas on these and similar subjects, may I not flatter myself that my ministry has not been wholly in vain?[5]

[4]Ralph Waldo Emerson, quoted in Arthur M. Schlesinger, *The American as Reformer,* Harvard, Cambridge, Mass., 1951, p. 3. With permission.
[5]Horace Mann, quoted in Merle Curti, *The Social Ideas of American Educators,* rev., Littlefield, Adams, Paterson, N.J., 1959, p. 108. With permission.

It was a time when many were convinced of their special cause and the absolute universality of their own analyses, and all seemed well prepared to march to the ramparts with stately banners flying; it was Quixotic perhaps, but energetic. "The United States . . . until very recent times has nearly always set the pace for the Old World in reform zeal. The outstanding exception has been in solutions for the social maladjustments arising from industrialization."[6] Unfortunately, the early educational-reform movement of Mann and others was not exempt from the exception that Schlesinger noted, for Mann's entire "ministry" is marked by uncertainty about socioeconomic issues and vacillation in response to opposition from the industrial establishment of his time.

Early nineteenth-century America, in the dawning of its industrial development and with its seemingly limitless frontier, was impatient to succeed, individually and collectively, and was often irritated by dreamers who questioned the orthodoxy of the evolving socioeconomic and political system and its religious underpinnings.

> To revise an old proverb, nothing sobers like success. The owner of property, however eager to improve society, has a personal investment in orderly change . . . No matter how desperate his [the American's] lot had been in Europe, he quickly displayed what impatient extremists despise as a middle-class attitude toward reform. Being surer of the future than of the present, he could not love innovation for its own sake, or be willing to risk all existing good in a general overturn. Hence he threw his weight on the side of piecemeal progress.[7]

More often than not, even that piecemeal progress had to be *safe*. It had to assure domestic tranquility so that growth would be undisturbed. The field of public education was no exception. Samuel Knox, in 1799, had made the issue clear.

[6]Schlesinger, op. cit., p. 5. With permission.
[7]Ibid., p. 8. With permission.

It is not, perhaps, possible to establish any system that can render education equally convenient and equally attainable by every individual of the nation in all their various situations and circumstances . . . In the present state of education however ably and successfully conducted in particular local situations, the nation is, in a great measure, incapable of judging its conditions or effects. Diversity of modes of education, also, tend, not only to confound and obstruct its operation and improvement, but also give occasion to many other inconveniences and disagreeable consequences that commonly arise in the various departments of civil society: or even the polished enjoyments of social intercourse. . . . In a country circumstanced and situated as the United States of America, a considerable local diversity in improvement, whether with respect to morals or literature, must be the consequence of such a wide extent of territory, inhabited by citizens blending together almost all the various manners and customs of every country of Europe. Nothing, then, surely, might be supposed to have a better effect toward harmonizing the whole in these important views than a uniform system of national education.[8]

The Knox theme of harmony and uniformity to counteract the dangers, inconveniences, and disagreeable consequences of diversity—a persistent theme throughout American educational history, and still present today—was obviously more popular than the reformers' notions of letting the free and heterogeneous democratic spirit flourish. Even Mann had reservations; he favored allowing only the safe and right in education. "All plans for reform and improvement," said the first educational reformer, "which appear to the eye of reason to be safe and useful, or which have been successfully tried elsewhere, are entitled to a fair trial among ourselves; and if they are found to pass this ordeal successfully, should be adopted."[9]

[8]Samuel Knox, quoted in Rena Vassar (ed.), *Social History of American Education,* Rand McNally, Chicago, 1965, vol. I, pp. 135–136.
[9]Curti, op. cit., p. 216. With permission.

Reform in education was obviously more rhetoric than action, but then this may be claimed as a valid general observation on all American reform; like the weather, reform is fun to talk about, but no one much wants to do anything about it. The good politician in America knows he must speak in general humanitarian, democratic, and social-justice language, but he also recognizes that, in order to stay elected to office, he must do as little as possible to implement his rhetoric, except when implementation either does not threaten vested interests or somehow can be manipulated by them to solidify or expand their security.

Action and commitment, the bywords of the youth of the seventies, have always been costly personally, and definitely not middle-class or genteel. Advocacy without action can be acceptable, even popular, but when advocacy demands disquieting personal action and its consequences, the fainthearted more often prevail. Schlesinger illustrates the choice, "When Emerson found Thoreau in Concord jail for refusing to pay a tax toward the support of what abolitionists regarded as a pro-slavery war on Mexico, the older man is said to have asked: 'Henry, why are you here?', and Henry to have replied, 'Waldo, why are you not here?'"[10]

Horace Mann was more Emerson than Thoreau, despite his admirable and tireless devotion to education. In his speeches and in his writings, he was quick to inquire into abuses and condemn them with fiery eloquence. Witness his attacks upon the rich in the following excerpts:

> The rich and strong live upon the poor and weak . . . as the great fishes eat up the little ones . . . The wealthy have more houses than they can live in, the costliest furniture, wardrobes, equipages, libraries, and all that art or nature can produce, while thousands of the children of the same Heavenly Father, around them, are houseless and shelterless, naked and hungry.

[10]Schlesinger, op. cit., p. 33. With permission.

> [Millionaires are] as dangerous to the welfare of the community, in our day, as was the baronial lord of the Middle Ages. Both supply the means of shelter and of raiment on the same conditions; . . . both use their superiority to keep themselves superior. The power of money is as imperial as the power of the sword; and I may as well depend upon another for my head as for my bread. The day is sure to come when men will look back upon the prerogatives of Capital, at the present time, with as severe and as just a condemnation as we now look back upon the predatory Chieftains of the Dark Ages.[11]

These were heady words, and should have earned Mann many a sworn enemy among the wealthy families of the day, such as the Appletons, Edward Dwight, the Lawrences, and the Lowells. But apparently they did not, for when Mann left the secretaryship of the Massachusetts State Board of Education, it was in response to a demand that he serve this same constituency in Congress. Subsequently there was considerable support in high places for Mann to run for governor, but he chose to go to Antioch College instead. Henry Barnard, Mann's reforming counterpart in Connecticut, was more prudent and openly advocated teaching the virtues of capitalism in schools; he also expressed his consistent religious orthodoxy, his friendship toward military institutions, and his defense of slavery. Barnard, considered the second greatest educational reformer of the day, began "his public career by denouncing Jackson . . . sharply condemning Jacksonian democracy for defaming the sacred judiciary and for its onslaughts against sound money and the national bank . . .[and] the protective tariff."[12]

But there were things to be changed, even if they were not to be reformed. Middle- and upper-class parents were expressing the usual worries about their teen-agers, and they saw in organized and universal public education the solution to their

---

[11]Curti, op. cit., pp. 115–116. With permission.
[12]Ibid., p. 145. With permission.

problems. As the nation became more preoccupied with mercantilism and industrialization, the family and church declined in importance as the all-pervasive socialization agents for children. The school was allowed to become the substitute, but the expectation of adherence to orthodoxy remained. Katz remarks that the educational-reform movement was

> spearheaded by the socially and intellectually prominent concerned for the preservation of domestic tranquillity and an ordered, cohesive society . . . joined and supported by middle-class parents anxious about the status of their children, and, somewhat tardily, for the most part, by organized schoolmen, who understandably enough have usually evaluated reform theory in terms of its impact upon their own precarious status.[13]

Certainly those early years had their tribulations with the young, echoed today in statements that are similar to the report of the Joint Committees of the City and County of Philadelphia, printed in the *Philadelphia Mechanic's Free Press* in 1830:

> There is one point in which the committees believe that the gradual extension and ultimate universal adoption of this [free school] system of education will produce a benefit, the value of which no human calculation can ascertain. It is but too well known that the growing effects of INTEMPERANCE—that assassinator of private peace and public virtue, are in this country terrific; and that this fearful pestilence, unless checked in its career by some more efficient remedy that has yet been resorted to, threatens to annihilate, not only the domestic peace and prosperity of individuals, but also the moral order and political liberties of the nation. No people can long enjoy liberty who resign themselves to the slavery of this tyrant vice. Yet does it appear to the committees, that all efforts to root this moral poison from the constitution of society will prove futile until the

[13]Katz, op. cit., pp. 213–214. With permission.

trial shall be made upon our youth. When we behold the hundreds, perhaps thousands of youth, who, between the ages of 14 and 21 are daily and nightly seduced around or into the innumerable dens of vice, licensed and unlicensed, that throng our suburbs, we are constrained to believe that in many if not in most cases, the unconquerable habit that destroys the morals, ruins the constitution, sacrifices the character, and at last murders both soul and body of its victim, is first acquired during the thoughtless period of juvenile existence. This plan of education, however, by its almost entire occupation of the time of the pupils, either in labor, study or recreations; by the superior facilities it affords for engrossing their entire attention, and by its capability of embracing the whole juvenile population furnishes, we believe, the only rational hope of ultimately averting the ruin which is threatened by this extensive vice.[14]

It would be difficult to understate the disappointment of some that neither the consequences envisioned in this report nor its advocated antidote ever came true. The drug culture of today—which poses the same threat—may at last succeed.

Perhaps one of the few truly activist reformers of the day was George Henry Evans, an ardent supporter of the anti-rent movement, the single tax, and what eventually became known as the Homestead Act. Evans was one of the chief organizers of the Workingman's party, and he edited the *Daily Sentinel, Young America,* and finally the *Workingman's Advocate,* which announced in 1829 the formation of the Association for the Protection of Industry and for the Promotion of National Education. The association's manifesto is clear enough; what is not clear is why George Henry Evans eventually abandoned his interest in education as a solution and turned exclusively to land reform to exercise his talents. When he did so, education was possibly robbed of a real activist who might have tested our theory of nonreform.

[14]Vassar, op. cit., pp. 180–181.

**ASSOCIATION FOR THE PROTECTION
OF INDUSTRY AND FOR THE PROMOTION
OF NATIONAL EDUCATION (1829)**

reasons for the formation of the association   Because industry is at present unprotected, oppressed, despised, and indirectly deprived of its just reward; and because there is in this republic no system of education befitting a republic; none which secures the equal maintenance, protection, and instruction of youth—of the children of the poor man as of the rich; none which is at once free from sectarian and clerical influences, and from aristocratical distinctions; none which is calculated to induce in the rising generation those habits of industry, those principles of sound morality, those feelings of brotherly love, together with those solid intellectual acquirements, which are necessary to secure to all the fair exercise of those equal political rights set forth in the institutions of the land.

means by which the association may attain the object   By procuring and publishing information as to the actual condition of the working class, and the actual remuneration for industry. By investigating the causes which depress industry and produce crime and suffering; and the measures which protect and favor industry, and which check oppression and vice.

By procuring information as to the state of public schools, as to the influence which rules them, and as to the value of the instruction they impart. By considering the practical means which are in the hands of the people to establish, through their representatives, a *state system of education.*

By printing and circulating tracts, calculated to give information to the people on these important subjects.

By corresponding regularly with similar societies in other towns and cities.

By promoting the gradual extension of the Association through all the states of the Union.

And, generally, by watching over the great interests of the people—a most necessary and most neglected duty; and by noting and proclaiming the influence, and opposing the success, of every measure that tends to injure or oppress them.

character of the association   It shall be such as to exclude no honest man. All who sign their names as members, shall be considered as having thereby expressed "THEIR INTENTION TO ASSIST IN DEFENDING THE RIGHTS AND PROMOTING THE INTERESTS OF THE PEOPLE, AND IN CARRYING through the state legislatures a system of equal republican education."

Although such an Association may expect to find the true friends of equal justice and popular instruction chiefly among the industrious classes, and may therefore reasonably be distrustful of others, it will not prejudge nor exclude any man, be his class what it may.

It will not meddle with speculative opinions; neither with religion, nor with irreligion. These are matters between each man and his own conscience. He who has faith, let him have it to himself; he who is religious, let him be religious in his closet when the door is shut, but not in public—not in an Association whose object is to discuss and reform temporal concerns. Plans for this world, and hopes of another, are two distinct things, that had better be kept separate; for men may agree about the one, while they will probably quarrel about the other.

State religion and monied ascendancy have done much harm to the people in every age and in every nation. It behooves an Association, therefore, which has in view the benefit of the people, to watch the political movements of the clergy and the rich. If the clergy, forgetting that they profess to be the servants of one whose kingdom is not of this world, intermeddle with temporal matters, a popular Association ought to thwart all such mischievous and unrepublican intermeddling. If the rich, presuming on their riches, attempt to carry measures *for* themselves and *against* the laboring classes, a popular Association ought to thwart all such mischievous and unrepublican attempts. But, though it be hard for a rich man, or for a clergyman, honestly to espouse the cause of the people against monied

203

and clerical oppression, the Association will exclude neither. Let both join it, if they see fit. Let both speak, if they will. If they speak well and advise aright, the people will be the gainers. If otherwise, the people are neither blind nor asleep, their eyes are open and their tongues are free: they can judge what is said, and they can reply to it.

The character of the Association, then, is *not exclusive and not sectarian*. It is NATIONAL.[15]

In contrast to the Workingman's party manifesto, the issue was joined in behalf of the vested social and economic interests in an editorial in the *Philadelphia National Gazette* in the following year, 1830.

It is a fundamental part of the Republican system to yield no power to government or to state except what is necessary—to leave as much as possible to individual enterprise and individual discretion;—to interfere only from imperative motives and for public ends of the highest and clearest utility, with the direction of private industry and the disposal of private fortune. Upon all this, the idea of committing to the state the regulation and care of the education of all citizens, with a uniform plan, is a broad encroachment,—a bold and momentous innovation. A number of the soundest and most patriotic thinkers, among us, might choose rather to assign to the state a general control over private property for any other object; or a multitude of parents would be glad to escape to any other land,—whatever might be the designation of its government, where they could enjoy at least freedom of choice as to the tuition of their children.[16]

What now emerges is that the early educational-reform movement, led by Mann, Barnard, and others, failed to recognize the social realities of their stratified society, a society in which the wealthy and powerful (and those who assumed that they would be

[15]Ibid., pp. 165–167.
[16]Ibid., p. 247.

someday) were reluctant to make any serious changes in the system, or in the social purposes of education, or their implementation. The reformers saw clearly that education and society were closely related, but they seemed unable to see the relationship as reciprocal. They understood that education could and did have a profound impact upon the society, but somehow they could not understand that the society had an equal or greater impact upon education, if only because education was a creation of that society and dependent upon it for its continued existence. As long as a reciprocal relationship is the reality (and one cannot readily foresee any change), public educators will be unable to initiate significant *social* change. It is possible, however, for educators to introduce some kinds of *educational* change. Attention must be drawn to the educational practices of the Oneida Community, which did vary from the public pattern. Children below age twelve virtually lived in their school (The Children's Wing) and were taught by a wide variety of persons. Since communality was a central value, education was seen as communal responsibility, meaning that all in the colony were considered to be both students and teachers. The Oneida Community amassed a rather large collection of books on a wide range of subjects, and the library was a central activity area. In short, everyone was to help everyone else improve his intellect. The success of the educational practices of the Oneida Community, as measured by subsequent college attendance, business success, and other activities, was quite remarkable. Evaluation of Oneida's education, however, was never systematic, and its temporary success could have been attributed to noneducational factors such as commitment to the colony itself as a motivating force. Its educational patterns were never adopted on any wide scale.[17]

Merle Curti, commenting on Mann's ultimate impact, states:

[17]See Constance Noyes Robertson, *Oneida Community: An Autobiography, 1851–1876,* Syracuse University Press, Syracuse, N.Y., 1970; Maren Lockwood Carden, *Oneida: Utopian Community to Modern Corporation,* Johns Hopkins, Baltimore, 1969.

Thus Mann was hardly free to think out either an educational or a social philosophy which would challenge the status quo in any fundamental way. He was free merely to attack certain features of the existing order—crime, ignorance, ill-health, pauperism, features which, he warned, were both a burden to tax payers and a menace to their interests. It was as if Mann were unconsciously trying to tell the dominant class what must be done to make its position more advantageous and secure.[18]

Later, Curti asserts:

Yet Horace Mann as an educator was bound in all he did, or permitted others to do, by the framework of the system in which he worked. That system, moreover, was responsible for the limitations which narrowed his vision and, even within the non-revolutionary area of reform, paralyzed his freedom of action in fighting *vested interests on which the schools depended for support.*[19] (Italics added.)

The Katz study's conclusions follow this same flow of thought, confirming the role of education as a nonreformer of society if such reforms are premised upon seriously changing the social purposes of education and the society that supports it.

By itself, education would not create the morality of an idealized countryside in the heart of the city; but this is a fact that mid-nineteenth century education promoters refused to see, and by refusing to see it they obscured the depth of social problems and became incapable of formulating effective strategies of social reform. Of course, they had reasons for their blindness. Aside from the educators themselves, the most vocal advocates of school reform were the very people providing the talent and money that helped usher in an industrial society. . . .

[18]Curti, op. cit., p. 131. With permission.
[19]Ibid., p. 138. With permission.

> When educational reform becomes too bound up with personal and group interests, it loses the capacity for self-criticism. It can be a dazzling diversionary activity turning heads away from the real nature of social problems. It can become a vested interest in its own right, so pious and powerful that it can direct public scorn to anyone who doubts. . . . Very simply, the extension and reform of education in the mid-nineteenth century were not a potpourri of democracy, rationalism, and humanitarianism. They were the attempt of a coalition of the social leaders, status-anxious parents, and status-hungry educators to impose educational innovation, each for their own reasons, upon a reluctant community. . . . We must face the painful fact that this country has never, on any large scale, known vital urban schools, ones which embrace and are embraced by the mass of the community, which formulate their goals in terms of the joy of the individual instead of the fear of social dynamite or the imperatives of economic growth. We must realize that we have no models; truly to reform we must conceive and build anew.[20]

"Building anew," of course, must be limited to educational change, lest we fall into the educator's old fantasy that education, as a dependent social institution, can initiate the reform of the total society.

The early educational-reform movement described by Katz was naive and stumbled over the social reality of public education's being a dependent social institution and therefore an illogical choice to lead socioeconomic or political reform. On the other hand, although the reform movement of the early twentieth century, largely associated with the progressive-education movement, was quite sophisticated, it made the same error. Perhaps the reformer is trapped by his own zeal into errors of omission; his fervor makes him overlook evidence that would dampen his ardor.

Some of the leaders of the twentieth century's first reform

[20]Michael B. Katz, *The Irony of Early School Reform,* Beacon Press, Boston, 1970, pp. 217–218. With permission.

movement recognized reality at first: They recognized that education could not reform society *at once;* it would take a generation or two of a new kind of generation to do the trick. Margaret Naumberg wrote in 1928:

> Any possibility of an immediate social or economic escape from the impasse of our civilization has become quite remote and rather absurd to me now. I've lived to see that whether people fought to save democracy or imperialism does not make the profound difference I had once hoped. I've wakened to a complete realization that all social and economic groups have identical methods of acting and reasoning, according to whether they are in or out of power.[21]

The answer then was to transform individuals in the hope that they would then reform the groups they joined as adults, perhaps a generation later. Deferred reform, however, is the meat of saints, not ordinary men and women, and just four years later, George S. Counts was trumpeting his famous challenge: "Dare the Schools Build a New Social Order?"[22]

The story of the earlier reform movement's inability to cope with a social and economic power structure that did not wish to be reformed repeated itself in the Progressive movement. The same issues confronted John Dewey, William Kilpatrick, George Counts, Harold Rugg, and the other giants in the nineteen-thirties and forties, who, it might be supposed, had the additional leverage working for them of public attention on growing business avarice and abuse and a depression with its attendant radicalism. Certainly the reformers sounded a fairly radical note. Consider the declaration of the *Social Frontier,* a journal representing these most powerful spokesmen of the Progressive era:

[21]Margaret Naumberg, quoted in Lawrence A. Cremin, *The Transformation of the School,* Knopf, New York, 1961, p. 212. With permission.
[22]George S. Counts, speech before the Progressive Education Association, Baltimore, 1932.

> In the years and decades immediately ahead, the American people will be called upon to undertake arduous, hazardous, and crucial tasks of social reconstruction. . . . In particular they must choose whether the great tradition of democracy is to pass away with the individualistic economy to which it has been linked historically or is to undergo the transformation necessary for survival in an age of close economic interdependence. . . . *The Social Frontier* assumes that the age of individualism in economy is closing and that an age marked by close integration of social life and by collective planning and control is opening.[23]

Such sentiments today would scare even the most liberal of politicians, and one can easily imagine them being greeted with outcries for immediate congressional investigations of the educational establishments, briefings by the FBI on all associated with the journal, as well as a few angry essays by William F. Buckley on the one hand, or a few apologies and reassurances from Arthur Schlesinger, Jr., on the other. For example:

> The assault on the educational system as a nursery of Communism and subversive doctrines is another danger to democracy. . . . After all, education is primarily an agency for transmitting tested knowledge. . . . If the public has any confidence at all in a profession which has always been outstanding for its loyalty, it will be content to let the members themselves expose any colleagues who abuse their trust. . . . Schools and colleges do not lack means of getting rid of such offenders. Therein lies the only rightful remedy.[24]

It is Cremin's judgment that the Progressive Education Association failed to reform, but its failure was "neither financial nor

[23]"Orientation," *The Social Frontier*, vol. 1, p. 4, October 1934.
[24]Arthur M. Schlesinger, *The American as Reformer,* Harvard, Cambridge, Mass., 1951, pp. 94–95. With permission.

philosophical, but ultimately political; it simply failed to comprehend the fundamental forces that move American education."[25] I would have to agree, but in doing so add that such forces were sociologically predictable.

One other restraining force with tremendous influence, operating beyond the broad undertow of socioeconomic and political conservatism in the power structure, seems incredibly obvious, so much so that it appears to be the proverbial individual tree one can so easily overlook while contemplating a forest. This force was, and still is, the mass of rank-and-file educators themselves, omnipresent, yet often ignored or brushed aside as if they did not really matter in the grand scheme of things.

Cremin starts to acknowledge the problem when he states:

> From the beginning, progressivism cast the teacher in an almost impossible role: he was to be an artist of consummate skill, properly knowledgeable in his field, meticulously trained in the science of pedagogy, and thoroughly imbued with a burning zeal for social improvement. It need hardly be said here as elsewhere on the pedagogical scene of the nineties, the gap between real and ideal was appalling.[26]

Entrance into the twentieth century did not change matters. Schoolmen and schoolmarms were not cast from such idealistic molds. Indeed, their occupation was, as Harold Laski once observed, "the last refuge of the shabby genteel."

As Louis Fischer and I have stated elsewhere:

> The distinctive American public school teacher who poked her head into the twentieth century schoolroom was . . . an (unfor-

[25]Cremin, op. cit., p. 273. With permission.
[26]Ibid., p. 168. With permission.

tunate) stereotype. Picture a woman, usually a maiden lady of undetermined age with a grim set line on her mouth and hard eyes, with hair neatly and tightly bound in a knot on her head. Despite the fact that she was usually young, public memory usually recalls her as old. Teachers are, to use an image from D. H. Lawrence, "odd wintry flowers upon a withered stem, yet new strange flowers." The alternative picture is that of an effusive, childless old woman who "just loves" every child; a "kissgranny or hugmoppet," in the words of James Thurber. In other words, the stereotype of the school teacher is pitiful and somewhat poignant. Teachers are lonely women who live in cramped apartments, with underwear and stockings drying in the bathroom. Their plan books have embroidered covers, and they are the humble, devoted servants of a community; but they have to go to the next town if they have a date. Each career is a private dedication, hampered by the necessity of Boy Scoutism and church decorum. Teachers are thought of as frightened people, eating cheerless meals in respectable diners, carrying on their mission in a world in which plumbing has surpassed poetry.[27]

We went on to say:

Socially, teachers were to remain, in a sense, second-class citizens, living under the close scrutiny of the public, often subjected to unreasonable restrictions on their private lives, and vulnerable to criticism at every turn. . . . The traditional values associated with their particular stratum both affect the operation of the schools and characterize the occupation of teaching.[28]

Wilbur Brookover suggested that teachers "so desire the

[27]Louis Fischer and Donald R. Thomas, *Social Foundations of Educational Decisions*, Wadsworth, Belmont, Calif., 1965, pp. 293, 308. With permission.
[28]Ibid., pp. 295, 310. With permission.

security, status and approval which those in control are in a position to give" that many "completely internalize the desires and beliefs of the controlling group."[29] Obviously, such people were not part of the reform crowd, even though they suffered, along with reformists, from what Katz calls "the mentality of cultural absolutism."

When Counts issued "Call to the Teachers of the Nation" in 1933,[30] it is not clear whether or not they were listening. Cremin observes: "It is difficult to assess the influence of the Counts Report. Redefer wrote years later that it caused little stir: teachers neither rose in revolt nor emancipated themselves from business control. Indeed, few of them read it in the first place."[31]

Similarly, *Social Frontier,* despite its all-star cast, "proved curiously ineffective in changing practice. . . . The gulf between theorist and practitioner was already widening in the educational profession, and the brilliant polemicists of the *Social Frontier* were simply finessed by less imaginative men with more specific pedagogical nostrums to purvey."[32] Cremin's depreciation of schoolmen to the contrary, the fact remains that the day-to-day operations of American education are moved in large part by its practitioners, who may be unglamorous as intellectuals, but who are, nevertheless, the soldiers who are held responsible for the ultimate success or failure of the system.

The sociology of practicing educators is not unknown. Waller contributed his classic and monumental study in 1932,[33] and Elsbree published his *The American Teacher* in 1939.[34] Myron Lieberman dealt extensively with such matters in *Education as a*

[29]Wilbur B. Brookover, *The Sociology of Education,* American Book, New York, 1955, p. 69.
[30]George S. Counts, "A Call to the Teachers of the Nation," *A Report of the Committee on Social and Economic Problems,* presented to the Progressive Education Association's Chicago Conference, 1933.
[31]Cremin, op. cit., p. 264. With permission.
[32]Ibid., p. 233. With permission.
[33]Willard Waller, *The Sociology of Teaching,* Wiley, New York, 1932.
[34]Willard S. Elsbree, *The American Teacher,* American Book, New York, 1939.

Profession in 1956.[35] I spoke to the point in an essay in 1958.[36] No studies published so far indicate that in attempting to reform education or, through it, a society one can afford to ignore the sociology of teachers and other educational professionals or the organizational contexts in which they work. Yet, surprisingly, Cremin did not mention either directly or in his supporting bibliographies any of the above studies or anyone else's more recent work. He too may have been blinded by the bright blaze and star fires of his own dreams of reform.[37]

The educational-reform movement that is brewing in the 1970s also reveals the errors of oversight. Again it must be said that if the lessons of history are to be learned, institutional education is not a likely direct avenue for reform of the society that supports it. The recent retaliations against universities in which students directed their actions at the outside supporting society should be example enough.

Hitchcock states: "In the main, the decline of the universities' fortunes is traceable . . . to the Right—politicians, taxpayers, and alumni who ultimately control the flow of funds and who, in increasing numbers, look upon such expenditures as either useless or counter-productive."[38]

But he goes on later to point out a further dilemma.

> But the reluctance of some conservative taxpayers and donors now to support institutions which they perceive as fostering

[35]Myron Lieberman, *Education as a Profession,* Prentice-Hall, Englewood Cliffs, N.J., 1956.

[36]Donald R. Thomas, "Who Wants To Be a Teacher?" *Teachers College Record,* vol. 60, no. 3, December 1958.

[37]Curiously, too, Katz's more recent volume, *School Reform: Past and Present,* Little, Brown, Boston, 1971, totally ignores the progressive-education era.

[38]James Hitchcock, "Colleges: No One Has a Good Word for Them," *New York Times,* May 23, 1971. Copyright © by the New York Times Company. Reprinted by permission.

values contrary to their own is being equaled by criticisms from the Left. . . . New Left ideology has been implicitly hostile to the universities, not only because of their alleged complicities with capitalism and the military but more importantly because, no matter how sincerely they may strive to achieve "open enrollment," for the foreseeable future at least they can scarcely help being elite institutions serving only a minority of the underpriviledged.[39]

It is not yet clear just how universities will survive these onslaughts, but in a world that increasingly demands more education for more people, it is probably premature to send for whom the bell tolls.

The reform of education, however, even to make it a more useful tool of social priorities, is possible so long as one takes into account the realities of the sociology of teachers and other professional educational workers. Since these realities may not be the same in the 1970s as they were in the 1930s and 1940s they must be researched: Who are our teachers? How do they live? How do they view the world and their work? How do they keep the educational ship afloat? Exhortation will not change them, as salesmen for the many recent federal programs and proclamations have learned. Witness the minimal impact of the Elementary and Secondary Education Act or the educational aspects of the war on poverty, just to name two examples of programs that had not done their sociological homework on the people who were supposed to make these programs succeed. Perhaps new training procedures that clearly promise prospective teachers new job satisfaction and public respect are in order. Perhaps reorganization of schools along more functional lines that include shared decision-making power between professionals and the community will evoke new responses. Perhaps a new breed of educator can be recruited. Perhaps expanded programs of research that will serve to professionalize education will

[39]Ibid. With permission.

cause change. There are dozens of changes and innovations that could conceivably lead toward reform, but they all must be rooted in the social realities.[40]

There is little doubt that reform is frustrated by the current deficit in school finances. As long as education is dependent upon local property taxes or minimal state supports, there will be serious questions about the ability of schools to engage in significant change. Not all of these questions will be legitimate; some fundamental organizational changes, many changes in educational intent, and some environmental redesign are not dependent upon additional monies. But balky schoolmen can claim with some justification that *major* overhauls of their systems must wait until massive infusions of funds are forthcoming. The redrafting of taxing policies then becomes prerequisite to educational change, innovation, and, ultimately, reform.

A second cause of resistance to reform lies in the fact that the traditional flow of American education, the ultimate achievement for Dick and Jane, has been graduation from a high-prestige college or university. The value assumption underlying this goal is the notion that Dick and Jane should enter the professional lifestyle, and in doing so, achieve the highest stratification level possible in the society. This has been the dream and it generally persists. The influence that colleges and universities wield upon the entire educational enterprise is incredible, not so much because of their intellectual contribution but because they are the carpeted entrance to first-class accommodations in the society.

Collegiate dominance of both the content and structure of secondary schools is well known. Colleges dictate courses (a structuring of knowledge), required credits, even specific content (via college aptitude, achievement, and entrance examinations) to which secondary schools must adhere, since the prestige system

[40]See "Teachers for the Real World," issued by the American Association of Colleges for Teacher Education in 1969 for one set of directions, particularly relating to the education of urban minority populations.

clearly awards highest honors to that high school which sends the most students to college. High verbal facility, which is the mask of the collegiate learning style, becomes the model for the secondary schools. Obviously then, elementary schools are expected to prepare young children to enter the high school with appropriate verbal skills, and the elementary program is designed and implemented accordingly. Rhetoric to the contrary, vocational education, distributive education, and all other non-college-bound tracks have always been considered second best and in an increasingly technological society, even that status is slipping. America is a highly stratified society; the competitive tradition could hardly have produced anything else. It is therefore naive to expect that education has evaded this reality. It seems more appropriate to acknowledge it and confront the implication that educational reform of the lower schools must await both the reform of the university and the prestige system that allows the university to dominate.

Control of the lower schools by the colleges is again obvious when one remembers that all certified school personnel are college trained; they cannot be licensed without such training. Teachers, counselors, and administrators are all enculturated with the biases of academia. The colleges not only tell them *what* to think, but *how* to think; thus even the most anticollegiate and disgruntled educator in the elementary and secondary schools cannot overcome his training. He may try to ignore it, but rarely does he offer a substitute for the college's traditional organization of knowledge or its basic transmission methodologies. Indeed, more often the lower-school educator even accepts the prestige system that says that the older the child he teaches, the wiser and more talented he must be.

Teacher and administrator training in colleges sustains its isolation from reform by hiding in the fortress of the collegiate prestige system and remaining structurally aloof from common pressure points that reformers might accost. The general public has no ready means to review collegiate education, nor do the lower schools, nor do the legislatures. They may suggest, but they have

virtually no way to enforce. Pragmatically, no reform can be successful unless it has the *power* to redistribute control of the schools.

We in the universities have been comfortable with these
arrangements, and have been dismayed by the efforts to reform our
contributions or to integrate us with reality.

A fourth deterrent to reform and even change or innovation is the growing influence of the educational "power broker." In
the wake of the Progressive Education Association, a significant
number of strategically placed educators were convinced that
political power was as crucial in the educational world as it was in
the world of politics and government, and certainly *more* important
than mere issues or programs. This new caste of mandarins in
education are educators whose subject matter specialty is knowing
the "right" people, knowing who is in what power position, what
power jobs are opening, and whom to see to get the largest grants.
Educational politicians and functionaries tend to protect and culti-
vate each other, particularly as education becomes increasingly
complex organizationally and therefore more political. Such protection occurs both inside institutional structures and without, and it can
even create new structures. The National Education Association, the
largest single educational organization in the country, for a long time
was accused and criticized for breeding a strong, interlocking
ingroup that was not always amenable to change, except when it was
on its own terms and tended to benefit the careers of its members,
particularly its paid leaders. The U.S. Office of Education has
sometimes practiced similar breeding methods. The NEA may still
have the problem, but the transient personnel of the USOE hardly
have time to nest.

The power brokers now emerge from the new fountains of
revenue and prestige: The private foundations, the federal government (U.S. Office of Education and other related agencies), and the
largest and most prestigious universities, just to name the most
obvious. Most programs of school innovation, change, or reform are
written to appeal to the funding reservoirs of these sources. Once the

money and prestige are dispensed, there is often little expectation that the promised changes will be achieved. In fact, more often than not, no one even asks. Reputations can be made on the basis of an untested but market-bright idea and the ability to obtain funding to try it. A university or school district can receive some much needed funds for the creation of a Center for the Study of Something or Other, and the power brokers thereby retain their influence. They make the decisions about who should be rewarded and are in a position to bestow the rewards through their network of positions on advisory commitees, consultantships, jobs to offer, speaking engagements available, national publications with pages that need filling, and a host of other techniques. Power brokers depend for their success upon the continuing existence of the rewards system they have erected. If the present demand for accountability were to be met, some educational empires would be toppled overnight.

There is further recalcitrance with which to contend in the dominions of school suppliers. Economic pressures to resist sweeping changes can be seen in the world of school-book publishing, for example, since any changes in instructional materials must first meet a sure marketability test before they will be produced. Production of new materials is at best slow, and the economic risks are real for publishers who must run the gauntlet of the school screening committees who make book-adoption decisions. School supplies tend to be standardized for mass markets, so that individualization is difficult. Suppose, for example, that a school district wanted text material, written at a twelve- or thirteen-year-old reading level, on the contribution of Serbo-Croatians to American life. Is it economically feasible for a publisher to attempt to meet this need? Many similar problems can be cited by producers of paper supplies, art materials, even maintenance equipment, to name but a few of the areas that constitute the billion-dollar school-supply industry.

It seems clear from the discussion of forces resisting reform that education is *not* a social revolutionary activity per se, and average educators have not been revolutionaries, nor is there any indication that they will soon be transformed. We find no evidence of any Joe Hills thus far in the history of American education, and the NEA or USOE are hardly offshoots of the Wobblies. It is traditional in the structure of this society that education should function as a reflection of the society, a transmitter of the culture, but not as the maker of that culture.

The problem of urban education then is reform but in a context that adequately reflects the realities of the changing social scene. To launder out the dysfunctionalism of educational organization and practice and to scrap the outmoded goal definitions and stultifying inbreeding are limited aspirations that could easily be coupled with a relentless drive for increased and earned professionalization. Just to accomplish these goals is challenge enough, and the accompanying slow accumulation of increments of change could eventually move American education in the direction of what might be its first true reform.

bibliography

Altshuler, Alan A.: *Community Control: The Black Demand for Participation in Large American Cities,* Pegasus Publishers, Western Publishing Company, Inc., New York, 1970.

Bennis, Warren G.: *Changing Organizations,* McGraw-Hill Book Company, New York, 1966.

————, Kenneth D. Benne, and Robert Chin: *The Planning of Change,* 2d ed., Holt, Rinehart and Winston, Inc., New York, 1969.

Biddle, William W. with Loureide J. Biddle: *The Community Development Process,* Holt, Rinehart and Winston, Inc., New York, 1965.

Bishop, Lloyd K.: *Individualizing Educational Systems,* Harper & Row, Publishers, Incorporated, New York, 1971.

Blau, Peter: *The Dynamics of Bureaucracy,* The University of Chicago Press, Chicago, 1955.

—— and W. Richard Scott: *Formal Organizations,* Chandler Publishing Company, San Francisco, 1962.

Brookover, Wilbur B.: *The Sociology of Education,* American Book Company, New York, 1955.

Bruner, Jerome S.: *The Process of Education,* Harvard University Press, Cambridge, Mass., 1961.

Cremin, Lawrence: *The Transformation of the School,* Alfred A. Knopf, Inc., New York, 1961.

Curti, Merle: *The Social Ideas of American Educators,* rev., Littlefield, Adams & Company, Paterson, N.J., 1959.

Demerath, N. J. and Richard A. Peterson: *System, Change, and Conflict,* The Free Press, New York, 1967.

Dentler, Robert A., Bernard Mackler, and Mary Ellen Warshauer: *The Urban R's,* Frederick A. Praeger, Inc., New York, 1967.

Dye, Thomas R. and Brett W. Hawkins: *Politics in the Metropolis,* Charles E. Merrill Books, Inc., Columbus, Ohio, 1967.

Elsbree, Willard S.: *The American Teacher,* American Book Company, New York, 1939.

Etzioni, Amitai: *Modern Organizations,* Prentice-Hall, Inc., Englewood Cliffs, N.J., 1964.

——: *A Comparative Analysis of Complex Organizations,* The Free Press, New York, 1961.

Fantini, Mario, Marilyn Gittell, and Richard Magat: *Community Control and the Urban School,* Frederick A. Praeger, Inc., New York, 1970.

Fava, Sylvia Fleis (ed.): *Urbanism in World Perspective,* Thomas Y. Crowell Company, New York, 1968.

Feldman, Saul D. and Gerald W. Thielbar: *Life Styles: Diversity in American Society,* Little, Brown and Company, Boston, 1972.

Fischer, Louis and Donald R. Thomas: *Social Foundations of Educational Decisions,* Wadsworth Publishing Company, Inc., Belmont, Calif., 1965.

French, Robert Mills (ed.): *The Community,* F. E. Peacock Publishers, Inc., Itasca, Ill., 1969.

Goodall, Leonard E.: *The American Metropolis,* Charles E. Merrill Books, Inc., Columbus, Ohio, 1968.

Goulet, Richard R.: *Educational Change: The Reality and the Promise,* Citation Press, New York, 1968.

Gross, Neal: *Who Runs Our Schools?* John Wiley & Sons, Inc., New York, 1958.

Gross, Ronald and Beatrice Gross (eds.): *Radical School Reform,* Simon & Schuster, Inc., New York, 1969.

Harrington, Michael: *The Other America,* Penguin Books, Inc., Baltimore, 1964.

Havighurst, Robert (ed.): *Metropolitanism: Its Challenge to Education,* 67th Yearbook of the National Society for the Study of Education, The University of Chicago Press, Chicago, 1968.

—— and Daniel Levine:*Education in Metropolitan Areas,* 2d ed., Allyn and Bacon, Inc., Boston, 1971.

Heller, Celia S. (ed.): *Structured Social Inequality,* The Macmillan Company, New York, 1969.

Hendrik, Irving G. and Reginald L. Jones: *Student Dissent in the Schools,* Houghton Mifflin Company, Boston, 1972.

Hillson, Maurice, Francesco Cordasco, and Francis P. Purcell (eds.): *Education and the Urban Community,* American Book Company, New York, 1969.

Hunter, Floyd: *Community Power Structure,* The University of North Carolina Press, Chapel Hill, 1953.

Hurwitz, Emanuel, Jr., and Robert Maidment (eds.): *Criticism, Conflict and Change,* Dodd, Mead & Company, Inc., New York, 1970.

Itzkoff, Seymour: *Cultural Pluralism and American Education,* International Textbook Company, Scranton, Pa., 1969.

Katz, Michael B.: (ed.): *School Reform: Past and Present,* Little, Brown and Company, Boston, 1971.

_____: *The Irony of Early School Reform,* Beacon Press, Boston, 1968.

Kramer, Judith R.: *The American Minority Community,* Thomas Y. Crowell Company, New York, 1970.

Kurokawa, Minako (ed.): *Minority Responses,* Random House, Inc., New York, 1970.

LaPiere, Richard T.: *Social Change,* McGraw-Hill Book Company, New York, 1965.

Larson, Calvin J. and Philo C. Wasburn (eds.): *Power, Participation and Ideology,* David McKay Company, Inc., New York, 1969.

Leonard, George B.: *Education and Ecstasy,* The Delacorte Press, New York, 1968.

Lieberman, Myron: *Education as a Profession,* Prentice-Hall, Inc., Englewood Cliffs, N.J., 1956.

Litt, Edgar: *Beyond Pluralism: Ethnic Politics in America,* Scott, Foresman and Company, Chicago, 1970.

Lowry, Ritchie P.: *Who's Running This Town?* Harper Torchbooks, Harper & Row, Publishers, Incorporated, New York, 1968.

Lukas, J. Anthony: *Don't Shoot, We Are Your Children,* Random House, Inc., New York, 1971.

Lynch, Kevin: *The Image of the City,* The M.I.T. Press, Cambridge, Mass., 1960.

March, James G. (ed.): *Handbook of Organizations,* Rand McNally & Company, Chicago, 1965.

Marris, Peter and Martin Rein: *Dilemmas of Social Reform,* Atherton Press, Inc., New York, 1967.

Mead, Margaret: *Culture and Commitment,* Natural History Press, Doubleday & Company, Inc., Garden City, N.Y., 1970.

Merton, Robert: *Social Theory and Social Structure,* The Free Press, New York, 1957.

———— et al. (eds.): *Sociology Today,* Basic Books, Inc., Publishers, New York, 1959.

Miles, Mathew (ed.): *Innovation in Education,* Bureau of Publications, Teachers College, Columbia University, New York, 1964.

Minar, David W. and Scott Greer (eds.): *The Concept of Community,* Aldine Publishing Company, Chicago, 1969.

Mumford, Lewis: *The City in History,* Harcourt, Brace & World, Inc., New York, 1961.

Olsen, Edward G. (ed.): *The School and Community Reader,* The Macmillan Company, New York, 1963.

Pettigrew, Thomas F.: *Racially Separate or Together?* McGraw-Hill Book Company, New York, 1971.

Postman, Neil, and Charles Weingartner: *The Soft Revolution,* Dell Publishing Co., Inc., New York, 1971.

————, and ————: *Teaching as a Subversive Activity,* The Delacorte Press, New York, 1969.

Reich, Charles: *The Greening of America,* Random House, Inc., New York, 1970.

Rogers, David: *110 Livingston Street,* Random House, Inc., New York, 1968.

Rose, Peter I.: *They and We,* Random House, Inc., New York, 1964.

Roszak, Theodore: *The Making of a Counter Culture,* Anchor Books, Doubleday & Company, Inc., Garden City, N.Y., 1969.

Schnore, Leo F.: *The Urban Scene,* The Free Press, New York, 1965.

Schwartz, Barry N. and Robert Disch: *White Racism,* Dell Publishing Co., Inc., New York, 1970.

Segal, Bernard E. (ed.): *Racial and Ethnic Relations,* Thomas Y. Crowell Company, New York, 1966.

Shibutani, Tamotsu and Kian M. Kwan: *Ethnic Stratification,* The Macmillan Company, New York, 1965.

Silberman, Charles E.: *Crisis in the Classroom,* Random House, Inc., New York, 1970.

————: *Crisis in Black and White,* Random House, Inc., New York, 1964.

Smith, B. Othanel, with Saul B. Cohen and Arthur Pearl: "Teachers for the Real World," American Association of Colleges for Teacher Education, Washington, D.C., 1968.

Spindler, George: *Education and Anthropology,* Stanford University Press, Stanford, Calif., 1955.

Suttles, Gerald D.: *The Social Order of the Slum,* The University of Chicago Press, Chicago, 1968.

Taylor, Harold: *Students Without Teachers,* McGraw-Hill Book Company, New York, 1969.

Thompson, James D.: *Organizations in Action,* McGraw-Hill Book Company, New York, 1967.

―――― (ed.): *Approaches to Organizational Design,* The University of Pittsburgh Press, Pittsburgh, 1966.

Vassar, Rena (ed.): *Social History of American Education,* vols. I and II, Rand McNally & Company, Chicago, 1965.

Waller, Willard: *The Sociology of Teaching,* John Wiley & Sons, Inc., New York, 1932.

Weinberg, Meyer: *Desegregation Research: An Appraisal,* Phi Delta Kappa, Bloomington, Ind., 1968.

Wilson, James Q. (ed.): *The Metropolitan Enigma,* Anchor Books, Doubleday & Company, Inc., Garden City, N.Y., 1970.